Focus in Grade 4
Teaching with Curriculum Focal Points

Focus in Grade 4

Teaching with Curriculum Focal Points

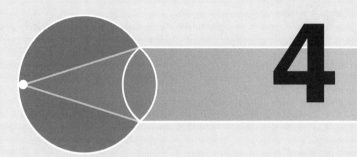

Jane F. Schielack, *Series Advisor*
Texas A&M University

NATIONAL COUNCIL OF
TEACHERS OF MATHEMATICS

Copyright © 2009 by
THE NATIONAL COUNCIL OF TEACHERS OF MATHEMATICS, INC.
1906 Association Drive, Reston, VA 20191-1502
(703) 620-9840; (800) 235-7566; www.nctm.org
All rights reserved

Library of Congress Cataloging-in-Publication Data

Focus in grade 4 / series advisor, Jane F. Schielack.
     p. cm. — (Teaching with curriculum focal points)
  Includes bibliographical references.
  ISBN 978-0-87353-627-1 (alk. paper)
 1. Mathematics—Study and teaching (Primary) —United States—Standards. 2. Fourth grade (Education) —
Curricula—United States—Standards. 3. Curriculum planning—United States—Standards. I. Schielack, Jane
F. II. National Council of Teachers of Mathematics. III. Title: Focus in grade four.
  QA135.6.F629 2009
  372.7'049—dc22
                         2009005752

The National Council of Teachers of Mathematics is a public voice of mathematics education, providing
vision, leadership, and professional development to support teachers in ensuring equitable mathematics
learning of the highest quality for all students.

Printed in the United States of America

Contents

Preface viii

Preface to *Curriculum Focal Points for Prekindergarten through Grade 8 Mathematics* ix

Acknowledgments x

1. Introduction 1

Purpose of This Guide 1

Purpose of Curriculum Focal Points 1

Impact of Focal Points on Curriculum, Instruction, and Assessment 2

Using This *Focus in Grade 4* Book...2

Bringing Focus into the Classroom: Instruction That Builds Understanding and Fluency..3

    An instructional progression approach...3

    In-depth instructional conversations 4

    Using mathematical drawings 4

An Important Grade 4 Issue: The Standard Algorithmic Approach to Multidigit Multiplication..5

2. Fluency in Whole-Number Multiplication 7

An Instructional Progression for Fluency in Multiplication 7

Early Foundations in Whole-Number Multiplication.......................9

Building Fluency in Multiplication 11

    Developing quick recall of multiplication and division facts 11

    Using place value with basic multiplication facts.....................................11

    The standard algorithmic approach to multidigit multiplication 12

    The collapsed method for recording multidigit multiplication...................18

    Estimation and fluency in multiplication 20

    Strengthening understanding of multiplication through problem solving.................20

Contents

Using multiplication to solve comparison (scalar) problems..................................20

Using multiplication to solve combination problems 21

Using problem solving to learn about remainders 22

Strengthening Fluency in Multiplication through Connections **23**

Connections in Later Grades................................**24**

Measuring Depth of Understanding................................**24**

3. Focusing on Fractions and Decimals 27

Instructional Progression for Connecting Fractions and Decimals 27

Early Foundations of Fractions................................27

Connecting Fractions and Decimals 32

Extending fraction concepts................................32

The relationship between improper fractions and mixed numbers................................36

Using fractions and whole-number place value to understand decimals................................38

Using fraction representations to interpret, visualize, and communicate about decimals................................41

Using fraction language to develop fluency in using decimals................................44

Identifying equivalent decimals................................45

Comparing and ordering decimals................................46

Strengthening Fluency through Connections................................48

Connections in Later Grades................................50

Measuring Depth of Understanding................................51

4. Focusing on Area of Two-Dimensional Shapes................................53

Instructional Progression for the Area of Two-Dimensional Shapes 53

Early Foundations 53

Early foundations for understanding two-dimensional shapes................................53

Early foundations for understanding area................................56

Contents

Building Understanding of Area 57

    The meaning of area as a measurable attribute....................................57

    Finding the area of rectangles 60

    Other units of area 62

    Strengthening understanding of area through problem solving 63

    Perimeter and area...67

Strengthening Fluency through Connections....................................69

    Transformations, symmetry, and congruence 69

    Composing and decomposing figures to compare their areas...................71

    Measuring and classifying angles 72

Connections in Later Grades...73

    Areas of parallelograms, triangles, and other polygons.........................73

    Surface area and volume 74

Measuring Depth of Understanding...75

References 76

On September 12, 2006, the National Council of Teachers of Mathematics released *Curriculum Focal Points for Prekindergarten through Grade 8 Mathematics: A Quest for Coherence* to encourage discussions at the national, state, and district levels on the importance of designing a coherent elementary school mathematics curriculum focusing on the important ideas at each grade level. The natural question that followed the release of *Curriculum Focal Points* was "How do we translate this view of a focused curriculum into the classroom?"

Focus in Grade 4, one in a series of grade-level publications, is designed to support teachers, supervisors, and coordinators as they begin the discussion of a more focused curriculum across and within prekindergarten through grade 8, as presented in *Curriculum Focal Points*. *Focus in Grade 4*, in conjunction with the *Focus in Grade 3* and *Focus in Grade 5* books, will provide a strong foundation to underlie the mathematics in a focused curriculum across grades 3 through 5. In addition, teacher educators should find *Focus in Grade 4* useful as a vehicle for exploring with their preservice teachers mathematical ideas and curriculum issues related to the suggested Grade 4 Curriculum Focal Points.

The contributors to, and reviewers of, these publications, all active leaders in mathematics education and professional development, guided the creation of this grade-level book as a framework for lesson-study experiences in which teachers deepen their understanding of the mathematical ideas they will be teaching. This book describes and illustrates instructional progressions for the mathematical concepts and skills of each Grade 4 Curriculum Focal Point, including powerful representational supports for teaching and learning that can facilitate understanding, stimulate productive discussions about mathematical thinking, and provide a foundation for fluency with the core ideas. Because these progressions cut across grades, the reader will see the same progressions for similar topics in grades 3, 4, and 5. Different parts of those progressions will appear as curriculum focal points in the different grades.

Whether you are working with your colleagues or individually, we hope you will find the discussions of the instructional progressions, representations, problems, and lines of reasoning valuable as you plan activities and discussions for your students and as you strive to help your students achieve the depth of understanding of important mathematical concepts necessary for their future success.

—Jane F. Schielack
Series Advisor

As states and local school districts implement more rigorous assessment and accountability systems, teachers often face long lists of mathematics topics or learning expectations to address at each grade level, with many topics repeating from year to year. Lacking clear, consistent priorities and focus, teachers stretch to find the time to present important mathematical topics effectively and in depth.

The National Council of Teachers of Mathematics (NCTM) is responding to this challenge by presenting *Curriculum Focal Points for Prekindergarten through Grade 8 Mathematics: A Quest for Coherence*. Building on *Principles and Standards for School Mathematics* (NCTM 2000), this new publication is offered as a starting point in a dialogue on what is important at particular levels of instruction and as an initial step toward a more coherent, focused curriculum in this country.

The writing team for *Curriculum Focal Points for Prekindergarten through Grade 8 Mathematics* consisted of nine members, with at least one university-level mathematics educator or mathematician and one pre-K–8 classroom practitioner from each of the three grade bands (pre-K–grade 2, grades 3–5, and grades 6–8). The writing team examined curricula from multiple states and countries as well as a wide array of researchers' and experts' writings in creating a set of focal points for pre-K–grade 8 mathematics.

On behalf of the Board of Directors, we thank everyone who helped make this publication possible.

Cathy Seeley
President, 2004–2006
National Council of Teachers of Mathematics

Francis (Skip) Fennell
President, 2006–2008
National Council of Teachers of Mathematics

Members of the Curriculum Focal Points for Grades PK–8 Writing Team

Jane F. Schielack, *Chair*, Texas A&M University, College Station, Texas
Sybilla Beckmann, University of Georgia, Athens, Georgia
Randall I. Charles, San José State University (emeritus), San José, California
Douglas H. Clements, University at Buffalo, State University of New York, Buffalo, New York
Paula B. Duckett, District of Columbia Public Schools (retired), Washington, D.C.
Francis (Skip) Fennell, McDaniel College, Westminster, Maryland
Sharon L. Lewandowski, Bryant Woods Elementary School, Columbia, Maryland
Emma Treviño, Charles A. Dana Center, University of Texas at Austin, Austin, Texas
Rose Mary Zbiek, The Pennsylvania State University, University Park, Pennsylvania

Staff Liaison
Melanie S. Ott, National Council of Teachers of Mathematics, Reston, Virginia

ACKNOWLEDGMENTS

The National Council of Teachers of Mathematics would like to thank the following individuals for developing a detailed outline of the content of this publication and for their reviews of, and feedback on, drafts of the manuscript. Special thanks go to Janie Schielack for all her time and support, her invaluable guidance and advice, and her continuing commitment to the Curriculum Focal Points project.

Jane F. Schielack
Series Advisor

Words & Numbers
Baltimore, Maryland
Content Development

Reviewers
John SanGiovanni
Howard County (Maryland) Public Schools

Thomasenia Lott Adams
University of Florida

Rose Mary Zbiek
Pennsylvania State University

Denny Gulick
University of Maryland

Michael Battista
Ohio State University

Purpose of This Guide

Your first question when looking at NCTM's Curriculum Focal Points might be, *How can I use NCTM's Focal Points with the local and state curriculum I am expected to teach?* NCTM's Curriculum Focal Points documents are not intended to be a national curriculum, but have been developed to help bring more consistency to mathematics curricula across the country. Collectively, they constitute a framework of how curricula might be organized at each grade level, prekindergarten through grade 8. They are also intended to help bring about discussion within and across states and school districts about the important mathematical ideas to be taught at each grade level. Because of the current variation among states' curricula, the Curriculum Focal Points are not likely to correlate perfectly with any one state curriculum. This volume explores the mathematics emphasized at grade 4 in the focused curriculum suggested by the NCTM Curriculum Focal Points framework. Additional grade-level and grade-band books are being developed by NCTM to help teachers translate the curriculum focal points identified for their grade level into coherent and meaningful instruction. Taken together, this grade 4 guide, along with the grade 3 and grade 5 guides and the grades 3–5 grade-band guide, can be used by groups of teachers in professional development experiences as well as by individual classroom teachers.

Purpose of Curriculum Focal Points

The mathematics curriculum in the United States has often been characterized as a "mile wide and an inch deep." Many topics are studied each year—often reviewing much that was covered in previous years—and little depth is added each time a given topic is addressed. In addition, because education has always been locally controlled in the United States, learning expectations can significantly differ by state and local school systems. NCTM's *Curriculum Focal Points for Prekindergarten through Grade 8 Mathematics: A Quest for Coherence* (2006) is the next step in helping states and local districts refocus their curricula. It provides an example of a focused and coherent curriculum in prekindergarten through grade 8 by identifying the most important mathematical topics, or "Focal Points," at each grade level. The Focal Points are not discrete topics to be taught and checked off, but rather a cluster of related knowledge, skills, and concepts. By organizing and prioritizing curriculum and instruction in prekindergarten through grade 8 around Focal Points at each grade level, teachers can foster more cumulative learning of mathematics by students, and students' work in the later grades will build on and deepen what they learned in the earlier grades. Organizing mathematics content in this way will help ensure a solid mathematical foundation for high school mathematics and beyond.

> *A curriculum is more than a collection of activities: It must be coherent, focused on important mathematics, and well articulated across the grades.*
>
> —The Curriculum Principle,
> *Principles and Standards for School Mathematics*

> The NCTM Curriculum Focal Points provide an example of a focused and coherent curriculum in prekindergarten through grade 8 by identifying the most important mathematical topics, or "Focal Points," at each grade level.

Prior to the Curriculum Focal Points, the National Council of Teachers of Mathematics (NCTM) began the process of bringing about change to school mathematics programs in the 1980s, particularly with the first document to outline standards in mathematics, titled *Curriculum and Evaluation Standards for School Mathematics* (NCTM 1989). This document provided major direction to states and school districts in developing their curricula. *Principles and Standards for School Mathematics* (NCTM 2000) further elaborated on the ideas of the 1989 Standards, outlining learning expectations in the grade bands of pre-K–2, 3–5, 6–8, and 9–12. *Principles and Standards* also highlighted six principles, which included the Curriculum Principle, to offer guidance for developing mathematics programs. The Curriculum Principle emphasized the need to link with, and build on, mathematical ideas as students progress through the grades, deepening their mathematical knowledge over time.

Impact of Focal Points on Curriculum, Instruction, and Assessment

Significant improvement can be made in the areas of curriculum, instruction, and assessment by identifying Focal Points at each grade level. At the curriculum level, Focal Points will allow for more rigorous and in-depth study of important mathematics at each grade level. This rigor will translate to a more meaningful curriculum that students can understand and apply. At the instructional level, Focal Points will allow teachers to more fully know the core topics they are responsible for teaching. Teachers will not necessarily be teaching *less* or *more* but will be able to teach *better*. Professional development can also be tailored to deepen teachers' knowledge of these Focal Points and connect these ideas in meaningful ways. Assessments can be designed that truly measure students' mastery of core topics rather than survey a broad range of disparate topics, thus allowing for closer monitoring of students' development. At the classroom-assessment level, having a smaller number of essential topics will help teachers have time to better determine what their students have learned and whether they have learned the material deeply enough to use and build on it in subsequent years. If state assessments are more focused as well, more detailed information can be gathered for districts and schools on areas for improvement.

Using This *Focus in Grade 4* Book

Many teachers tell us that they did not have an opportunity in their teacher-preparation programs to build sufficient understanding of some of the mathematical topics that they now teach. The discussion of the mathematical ideas presented here is detailed enough for teachers to begin building understanding of the mathematics contained in each grade 4 Focal Point. To further understand what mathematics students are expected to learn before grade 4 and in later grades, teachers would also benefit from examining the publications *Focus in Grade 3* (NCTM 2009) and *Focus in Grade 5* (NCTM 2009). We suggest that teachers form study groups (such as those in lesson study or mathematics circles or other learning communities) to read and discuss parts of this publication, to work together to build a deeper understanding of the mathematical topics in each Focal Point, and to plan how to help their students develop such understanding by adapting as needed their present grade 4 teaching and learning strategies and materials. A helpful approach for other teacher working groups has been to share students' insights and questions and to look at students' work to understand different ways that students use to solve problems, to address errors, and to help move students forward in a progression that fosters both understanding and fluency. Because educators' lives are busy and demanding, a teacher is better served by concentrating on small portions of this publication at a time and working through them deeply instead of trying to do too much at once and getting discouraged. Teachers' learning, like students' learning, is a continuous process that can be very rewarding.

Bringing Focus into the Classroom: Instruction That Builds Understanding and Fluency

Although the main goal of this publication is to present in more detail the mathematics in each of the Focal Points, some important pedagogical issues also need to be taken into account when creating an environment that supports focused instruction. Pedagogical principles for classroom teachers that do help students build understanding are outlined in *Principles and Standards for School Mathematics* (NCTM 2000) and the National Research Council reports *Adding It Up* (Kilpatrick, Swafford, and Findell 2001) and *How Students Learn: Mathematics in the Classroom* (Donovan and Bransford 2005). An instructional environment that supports the development of understanding and fluency needs to be based on a logical progression of content that is connected across grades as well as within grades, should provide opportunities for students and teachers to engage in mathematically substantive discussions, and should involve teachers and students in the interpretation and creation of mathematical representations to enhance their understanding.

An instructional progression approach

An instructional progression of concepts and skills supports coherence across and within grades. The table at the beginning of each Focal Point that outlines the instructional progression presents the mathematics suggested for grade 4 within the context of the mathematics suggested for the grades immediately before and after it. Teacher study groups can work to identify gaps in the knowledge of their students that might be causing them difficulties with the grade 4 mathematics. In addition, the instructional progression provides a view of the future mathematics in which students will be applying their grade 4 knowledge and skills.

In-depth instructional conversations

Students have little opportunity to build understanding in a classroom in which the teacher does all the talking and explaining. A valuable instructional approach is one in which teachers create a nurturing, meaning-making community as students use "math talk" to discuss their mathematical thinking and help one another clarify their own mathematical thinking, understand and overcome errors, and describe the methods they use to solve problems (Fuson and Murata 2007). Such discussions identify commonalities and differences and advantages and disadvantages across methods. By having students talk about their informal strategies, teachers can help them become aware of, and build on, their implicit informal knowledge (Lampert 1989; Mack 1990). As the teacher and students learn to listen respectfully to the "math talk" of others, they model, structure and clarify, instruct or explain, question, and give feedback to further one another's learning. As students' understanding and fluency in various topics increase, the amount and type of class discussion related to each topic will change. In-depth discussion on new topics should begin as more sophisticated, mature discussion of previously encountered topics continues.

Using mathematical drawings

The use of mathematical representations, in particular mathematical drawings, during problem-solving discussions and explanations of mathematical thinking helps listeners better understand the speaker. The use of mathematical drawings as a component of homework and classwork by both students and teachers helps them better understand one another's thinking and thus provides continual assessment to guide instruction as the teacher addresses issues that arise in such drawings and accompanying talk (e.g., errors or interesting mathematical thinking). Mathematical drawings, rather than show situational details of the real objects involved, focus on the mathematically important features and relationships in the situation, such as the quantities and operations, and can involve small circles or other simple shapes to represent a variety of objects. Such representations of individual objects then can evolve into schematic numerical drawings that show relationships between, or operations on, numbers rather than show all the individual objects. Examples of mathematical drawings that can be produced and understood by students are used throughout this publication.

An Important Grade 4 Issue: The Standard Algorithmic Approach to Multidigit Multiplication

The Curriculum Focal Points specify topics for which students should achieve fluency with *the standard algorithm*. By this phrase, mathematicians mean *the standard algorithmic approach* that involves certain basic mathematical properties and not the specific ways in which numerals are written to show the steps in applying these properties. For example in grade 4, students learn that *the standard algorithmic approach* for multidigit multiplication involves using the distributive property to multiply each digit and its accompanying power of 10 in one factor by each digit and its accompanying power of 10 in the other factor and then adding the "partial products." Simpler and more complex ways can be used to record this same process. Each way has advantages and disadvantages, and students should discuss the relative merits and shortcomings of each way of recording.

Adding It Up (NRC 2001) clarified that in fact no such thing as *the* standard algorithm exists. Many different algorithms (systematic methods of repeated steps for carrying out a computation) have been used over time in the United States, and many different algorithms are used presently in other countries. Students from other countries may bring such written methods into a classroom in the United States. Students from the United States will often bring the current common methods learned from experiences at home. Selected methods need to be discussed and related to mathematical drawings or other representations so that the selected methods can be understood. A student should be allowed to use any method that is mathematically desirable and that the student can explain. Mathematically desirable methods use *the standard algorithmic approach* and therefore meet any state goal that requires use of *the standard algorithm*. Some mathematics programs suggest that students not use a particular shortened algorithm because it often involves a complex way of recording, but this method will come from some homes and does need to be included in the class discussion. The discussion should emphasize that the steps and the meanings underlying any methods of recording are the important features, and understanding these features—why the methods of recording work mathematically—is a major focus of developing computational fluency.

The three grade 4 Focal Points and their Connections are reproduced on the following page.

Curriculum Focal Points and Connections for Grade 4

The set of three curriculum focal points and related connections for mathematics in grade 4 follow. These topics are the recommended content emphases for this grade level. It is essential that these focal points be addressed in contexts that promote problem solving, reasoning, communication, making connections, and designing and analyzing representations.

Grade 4 Curriculum Focal Points

Number and Operations and Algebra: Developing quick recall of multiplication facts and related division facts and fluency with whole number multiplication

Students use understandings of multiplication to develop quick recall of the basic multiplication facts and related division facts. They apply their understanding of models for multiplication (i.e., equal-sized groups, arrays, area models, equal intervals on the number line), place value, and properties of operations (in particular, the distributive property) as they develop, discuss, and use efficient, accurate, and generalizable methods to multiply multidigit whole numbers. They select appropriate methods and apply them accurately to estimate products or calculate them mentally, depending on the context and numbers involved. They develop fluency with efficient procedures, including the standard algorithm, for multiplying whole numbers, understand why the procedures work (on the basis of place value and properties of operations), and use them to solve problems.

Number and Operations: Developing an understanding of decimals, including the connections between fractions and decimals

Students understand decimal notation as an extension of the base-ten system of writing whole numbers that is useful for representing more numbers, including numbers between 0 and 1, between 1 and 2, and so on. Students relate their understanding of fractions to reading and writing decimals that are greater than or less than 1, identifying equivalent decimals, comparing and ordering decimals, and estimating decimal or fractional amounts in problem solving. They connect equivalent fractions and decimals by comparing models to symbols and locating equivalent symbols on the number line.

Measurement: Developing an understanding of area and determining the areas of two-dimensional shapes

Students recognize area as an attribute of two-dimensional regions. They learn that they can quantify area by finding the total number of same-sized units of area that cover the shape without gaps or overlaps. They understand that a square that is 1 unit on a side is the standard unit for measuring area. They select appropriate units, strategies (e.g., decomposing shapes), and tools for solving problems that involve estimating or measuring area. Students connect area measure to the area model that they have used to represent multiplication, and they use this connection to justify the formula for the area of a rectangle.

Connections to the Focal Points

Algebra: Students continue identifying, describing, and extending numeric patterns involving all operations and nonnumeric growing or repeating patterns. Through these experiences, they develop an understanding of the use of a rule to describe a sequence of numbers or objects.

Geometry: Students extend their understanding of properties of two-dimensional shapes as they find the areas of polygons. They build on their earlier work with symmetry and congruence in grade 3 to encompass transformations, including those that produce line and rotational symmetry. By using transformations to design and analyze simple tilings and tessellations, students deepen their understanding of two-dimensional space.

Measurement: As part of understanding two-dimensional shapes, students measure and classify angles.

Data Analysis: Students continue to use tools from grade 3, solving problems by making frequency tables, bar graphs, picture graphs, and line plots. They apply their understanding of place value to develop and use stem-and-leaf plots.

Number and Operations: Building on their work in grade 3, students extend their understanding of place value and ways of representing numbers to 100,000 in various contexts. They use estimation in determining the relative sizes of amounts or distances. Students develop understandings of strategies for multidigit division by using models that represent division as the inverse of multiplication, as partitioning, or as successive subtraction. By working with decimals, students extend their ability to recognize equivalent fractions. Students' earlier work in grade 3 with models of fractions and multiplication and division facts supports their understanding of techniques for generating equivalent fractions and simplifying fractions.

Reprinted from *Curriculum Focal Points for Prekindergarten through Grade 8 Mathematics: A Quest for Coherence* (Reston, Va.: National Council of Teachers of Mathematics, 2006, p. 16).

2 Fluency in Whole-Number Multiplication

The focus in grade 4 is on developing fluency in basic multiplication and related division facts, as well as fluency in using whole-number multiplication of multidigit numbers. Students can build on the knowledge of basic facts that they learned in grade 3 to enhance automaticity for single-digit facts and to multiply multidigit numbers in grade 4. By using visual representations of the distributive property of multiplication over addition along with increasingly more efficient numerical representations of the processes involved in multiplying multidigit numbers, students can build understanding that leads to fluency in using the standard algorithmic approach for multidigit multiplication. We briefly discuss the concepts and skills that students focus on in grade 3 that prepare them to be successful in multidigit multiplication in grade 4. We also discuss how understanding of, and fluency in, whole-number multiplication is an important foundation for understanding multidigit division in grade 5.

An Instructional Progression for Fluency in Multiplication

The focus on fluency in multiplication in grade 4 is supported by a progression of related mathematical ideas before and after grade 4, as shown in table 2.1. To give perspective to the grade 4 work, we first discuss some of the important ideas that students focused on in grade 3 that prepared them for expanded work with multiplication in grade 4. At the end of the detailed discussion of this grade 4 Focal Point, we present examples of how students will use their understandings of, and skills with, multiplication in later grades. For more detailed discussions of the "before" and "after" parts of the instructional progression, see the appropriate grade-level books, that is, *Focus in Grade 3* (NCTM 2009) and *Focus in Grade 5* (NCTM 2009).

Table 2.1 represents an instructional progression for the understanding of whole-number multiplication in grades 3 through 5.

Table 2.1
Grade 4: Focusing on Fluency of Whole-Number Multiplication
Instructional Progression for Developing Understanding in Grades 3–5

Grade 3	Grade 4	Grade 5
Students use equal-group, array, and area situations and models to represent and interpret multiplication and division and their relationship. Students use multiplication and division to solve problems. Students connect skip counting with the multiples of a number. Students use patterns in lists of multiples, e.g. in a multiplication table, to learn basic facts. Students use properties of addition and multiplication (e.g., commutative, associative, and distributive properties) and known facts to find related unknown facts. Students use the mathematical relationship between multiplication and division to view "finding a quotient" as "finding an unknown factor."	Students work toward quick recall of basic multiplication facts and related division facts Students expand their application of multiplication and division to solve problems, including those involving scalar comparison and combination situations. Students use their knowledge of multiples to extend whole-number division to include division with remainders.* Students use place-value patterns to find multiples of tens, hundreds, and thousands. Students apply their understanding of representations for multiplication (i.e., equal groups, arrays, area models, and scalar comparisons) and their knowledge of basic facts, place value, and the distributive property to multiply multidigit numbers. Students use properties of multiplication and patterns in place value to estimate and calculate products mentally. Students use properties to apply the standard algorithmic approach to multiplication with multidigit numbers and use this approach to solve problems.	Students apply their understanding of models for division (e.g. arrays, area models), place value, properties, and the relationship of division to multiplication as they develop efficient procedures to find quotients involving multidigit dividends.* Students use their understanding of multiplication and its relationship to division to estimate and calculate quotients mentally. Students learn and understand the standard algorithmic approach to division involving multidigit dividends and use this approach to solve problems. Students consider a context in which a problem is presented to select the most useful form of the quotient, and then interpret it appropriately. Students use their understanding of factors and multiples to explore prime and composite numbers, common factors, and common multiples.**

* Also appears in Grade 4 Connections to the Focal Points
** Appears in the Grade 5 Connections to the Focal Points

Early Foundations in Whole-Number Multiplication

In grade 3, students learn the meaning of multiplication as the joining of equal groups. Students learn that 3 × 4 means 3 groups of 4 or 4 taken 3 times. This expression can also mean 4 groups of 3 or 3 taken 4 times. Even though 3 groups of 4 or 4 groups of 3 are physically different, students encounter situations in grade 3 that illustrate that because of the commutative property, the product is the same no matter which factor represents the groups and which factor represents the quantity in each group. In grade 3, when working only with whole numbers, students use equal groups, arrays, and area models to demonstrate commutativity as an important property of multiplication.

When working with the equal-groups model in grade 3, students model 3 × 4 by drawing three groups with four objects in each group. They count all the objects to find the product. Because the total is twelve objects, 3 × 4 = 12. Students then move to a more efficient representation of writing the number 4 in each group, then skip counting by 4 to determine the product, as shown in figure 2.1.

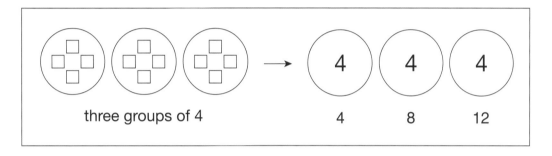

Fig. 2.1. Progression of representing the equal-groups model

When using the array model in grade 3, students use equal rows and columns to show the number of equal groups and the number in each group represented by the factors in a multiplication problem. The product is the total number of objects in the array. Grade 3 students progress from counting all the objects in an array to multiplying the number of rows by the number of columns, or vice versa, to find the total number of objects. Figure 2.2 shows an array model for 3 × 4 = 12.

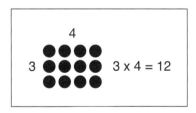

Fig. 2.2. An array model

The model of multiplication that students use in grade 3 is a connected array, or area, model which appears as a rectangle divided into squares of equal size. The equal number of squares in each row connects back to the meaning of multiplication as the joining of equal groups and is like an array of squares with equal rows and equal columns. Students see that 3 rows of 4 square units is a situation involving 3 groups of 4, or a representation of 3 × 4, as shown in figure 2.3.

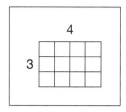

Fig. 2.3. Area model of multiplication as a connected array of squares

Students in grade 3 also use area models to illustrate the distributive property of multiplication over addition as a strategy for using known products to find unknown products. For example, figure 2.4 shows a model of 7 × 8. Because 7 can be thought of as 5 + 2, the area model is divided into two sections: one section that represents 5 × 8 and another section that represents 2 × 8. Students multiply to find the number of squares in each of the parts, then add the parts to get 56. If students know the products 5 × 8 and 2 × 8, this strategy is more efficient than counting the individual squares in a 7 × 8 model to find the product of 56.

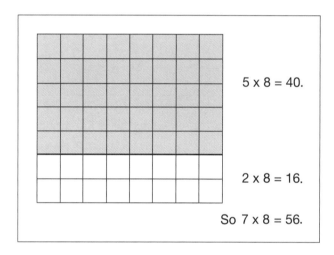

Fig. 2.4. An area model for using known products to find an unknown product

These visual representations, along with the number line, are all used in grade 3 to help form the foundation for understanding the meaning of multiplication. Once students have internalized the meaning of multiplication and some of its properties, they have the foundation to begin developing the basic multiplication facts in a meaningful way and to move into applying these concepts in grade 4 to multi-digit multiplication.

As students in grade 3 work on understanding the meaning of multiplication ideas, they also are encountering examples of the mathematical relationship between multiplication and division. Whereas multiplication can be represented by joining equal groups, division can be represented by separating a quantity into equal groups. If students are asked to identify the meaning of 6 × 3 = 18, they should understand that "6 groups of 3 are 18 in all." As students develop an understanding of division's relationship to multiplication, they need to identify the meaning of 18 ÷ 6 as the total 18 separated into equal groups of 6 or 6 equal-sized groups. In other words, 18 ÷ 6 represents the number n such that $n × 6 = 18$. This understanding of the mathematical relationship between division and multiplication leads students to the knowledge that, if they know the multiplication facts, they actually already know the related division facts. For example, if students know that $8 \times 5 = 40$ and $5 \times 8 = 40$, and they know that $40 \div 5 = n$ such that $n \times 5 = 40$, then they know that $40 \div 5 = 8$ and $40 \div 8 = 5$. Students begin to realize that the product in a multiplication fact becomes the dividend in the related division fact and that the factors become the divisor and quotient.

Building Fluency in Multiplication

Developing quick recall of multiplication and division facts

Students in grade 4 continue to use the variety of strategies that they were introduced to in grade 3 to make sense of and learn the multiplication facts. These strategies include exploring patterns in skip counting and place value, as well as creating visual representations that help students apply multiplicative properties to use products they know to find those they do not know. (See *Focus in Grade 3* [NCTM 2009] for more details on these strategies.) However, in grade 4, we want to help students realize that expanding the number facts they understand *and* "just know rapidly" helps them become more efficient in multiplying multidigit numbers. Students' success in mathematical content they encounter in later grades is enhanced by their ability to quickly recall basic multiplication and division facts. With this automaticity, the basic facts become tools that students can use to solve more difficult problems involving multiplication or division.

Using place value with basic multiplication facts

Understanding place value will help students apply their knowledge of basic facts to find products involving powers of 10. Knowledge of extended facts that involve multiples of tens, hundreds, and so on is a crucial component of understanding multidigit multiplication.

Figure 2.5 illustrates area and array models that can help students understand and generalize the patterns involved with multiplying by 10, 100, and 1000. Note that students' knowledge of place value allows them to compose and decompose numbers and, specifically, partition numbers into hundreds, tens, and ones, to fully comprehend the multiplication shown in the examples related to the basic fact $3 \times 2 = 6$.

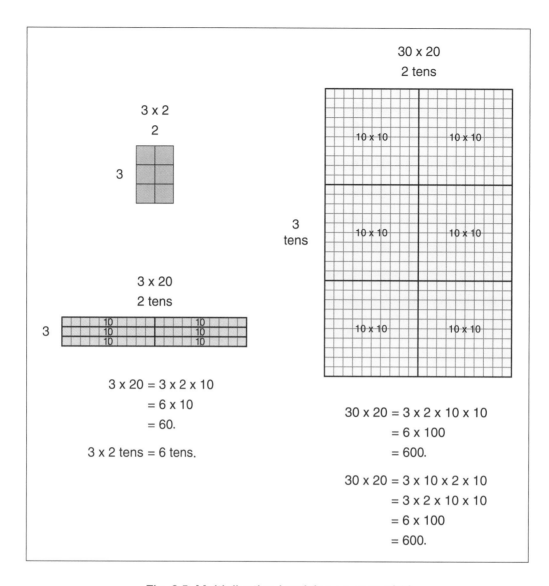

30 x 20

2 tens

3 x 2

2

3

3 x 20

2 tens

3

3
tens

3 x 20 = 3 x 2 x 10

= 6 x 10

= 60.

3 x 2 tens = 6 tens.

30 x 20 = 3 x 2 x 10 x 10

= 6 x 100

= 600.

30 x 20 = 3 x 10 x 2 x 10

= 3 x 2 x 10 x 10

= 6 x 100

= 600.

Fig. 2.5. Multiplication involving powers of 10

The standard algorithmic approach to multidigit multiplication

For students to develop understanding of procedures for multiplying multidigit numbers, the array and area models are particularly powerful and can be used systematically to help students develop the standard algorithmic approach to multidigit multiplication. From the beginning of the development with this model, students can see why and how we multiply each place in one number by each place in the other number. This is the big idea behind the standard algorithmic approach to multidigit multiplication; it uses the distributive property of multiplication over addition. Students have worked with the distributive property in developing and using strategies for the greater single-digit products when thinking $7 \times 8 = (5 \times 8) + (2 \times 8) = 40 + 16 = 56$. As students encounter this property and the area model as unifying threads, they will be encouraged to develop efficient, accurate, and generalizable methods for recording the mathematics involved in the multiplication of multidigit numbers.

Many people understand "the standard multiplication algorithm" to mean a specific way of recording the numerical steps of a multidigit multiplication problem. However, from a purely mathematical perspective, where or how the big ideas of an algorithm are recorded does not matter, because the ordered set of big ideas themselves constitutes the algorithm. At the same time, from the perspective of learning and understanding, where or how the steps of an algorithm are recorded can be crucially important. Therefore, we use the phrase *standard algorithmic approach to multidigit multiplication* to incorporate the collection of all sensible ways of showing or recording the steps of a mathematically desirable procedure for multiplying multidigit factors. Thus, students can use the properties of the numbers and operations and record the mathematical ideas involved in the standard algorithmic approach to multidigit multiplication in ways that make sense to them. This perspective recognizes that the steps and the logic of an algorithm are at the heart of the algorithm, not the particular method of recording it. The following models and descriptions show pictorial methods that depict the standard algorithmic approach to multidigit multiplication and progressively more efficient ways to record the multiplication process.

One pictorial method for representing multiplication that students are already familiar with is a connected array, or area, model. A connected array is a powerful model for multidigit multiplication in grade 4 because it can show very clearly the partial products resulting from separately multiplying the digits in the different place-value positions. Figure 2.6 shows an area model for the multiplication problem 4 × 17. The diagram shows 4 rows of 17 as separated into 4 rows of 10 and 4 rows of 7. By joining the 4 tens into 40 and the 4 sevens into 28, students find that 4 groups of 17 is a total of 40 + 28, or 68.

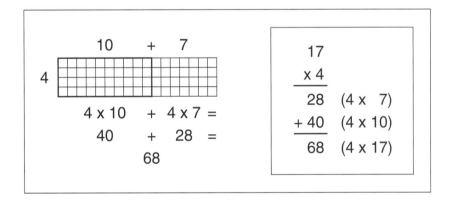

Fig. 2.6. A connected array, or area, model representing partial products for 4 × 17

As students count the tens and ones shown in an area model and record their findings using symbols, they begin to see the connection between their recording of tens and ones and the distributive property of multiplication over addition (see the equations below the array in fig. 2.6). The partial products created from the distributive property of multiplication over addition can also be recorded in a vertical format, as shown in the box at the right in figure 2.6.

The model in figure 2.6 shows that breaking a two-digit factor into tens and ones and applying the distributive property of multiplication over addition is a useful strategy for multidigit multiplication. This strategy can be further developed for multiplying two two-digit numbers, as presented in the following classroom discussion.

Teacher: We used connected arrays to show multiplication of a two-digit number times a one-digit number. We can use the same type of model to show multiplication of two two-digit numbers, for example 24 × 37. If we use dot paper, we can use the dots to show the corners of all the squares that we would need in the connected array of 24 rows of 37 squares. I'm going to draw some lines in the array, like we've done with other array models, to show the whole product separated into parts that are easier to think about. [See fig. 2.7.]

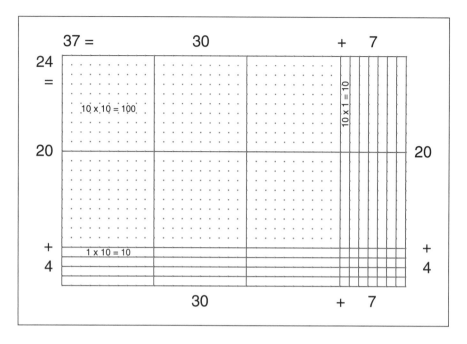

Fig. 2.7. Teacher-drawn dot array to show 24 × 37

Teacher: Would anyone like to tell me what you see in this model?

Talia: I see things that look like place-value blocks—the parts labeled 10 × 10 look like hundred squares. And the ones labeled 1 × 10 look like the tens pieces.

Greg: That's why it makes sense to write 10 × 10 = 100 in the squares—they're 100. And the 1 × 10 pieces are 10. And those little squares in the corner are the ones.

Teacher: So, what does this picture tell us about the product 24 × 37?

Armand: If you count all the different parts, then 24 × 37 is 6 hundreds plus 26 tens plus 28 ones.

Teacher: Who would like a more efficient way to figure out 24 × 37? [Everyone raises his or her hand.] Here is a way that we can draw the connected array to help us pay attention to the important parts of the product. [See fig. 2.8.] See how these parts are like the parts in the more complicated picture, and like the pieces that Armand counted? We show 37 as 30 + 7 and 24 as 20 + 4, just like in the connected array, but without all the extra dots and lines. Then, the large rectangle part represents 2 tens × 3 tens, or 6 hundreds. The medium-rectangle parts represent 4 × 3 tens, or 12 tens, and 7 × 2 tens, or 14 tens. Armand counted 26 tens altogether in the other picture, and 12 tens and 14 tens makes 26 tens. Finally, the small rectangle represents 4 ones × 7 ones, or 28 ones. How do we find the total product?

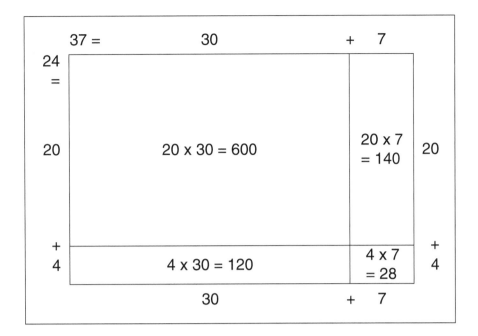

Fig. 2.8. Teacher's drawing to emphasize important parts of the array model for 24 × 37

Terry: Add up all the parts! We could write the math beside the picture like this [fig. 2.9]:

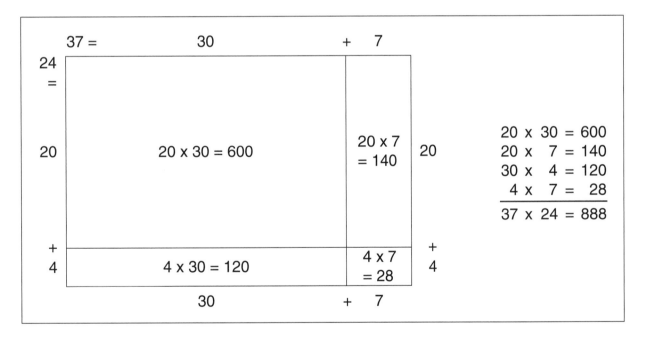

Fig. 2.9. Student's recording of the mathematics next to the array model for 24 × 37

Teacher: That is a nice way to keep track of all of the partial products. If we could do this without drawing a picture, it would be even more efficient.

[With more examples and more discussion, the students come to see that they can use symbols in several ways to determine and record the partial products in multidigit multiplication.]

Teacher: I see that you have all had to think about place value a lot when doing these partial products. Let's talk about some of the ways you have used to record the math you are doing when you multiply with two-digit numbers.

Selina: I started out needing to write down all of the parts so I could see the place values and not forget any of the multiplications. And, if I did the biggest part first, it was easier to keep the places lined up. Like this:

$$
\begin{array}{r}
37 = 30 \times 7 \\
\underline{\times\ 24 = 20 \times 4} \\
20 \times 30 = 600 \\
20 \times\ \ 7 = 140 \\
4 \times 30 = 120 \\
\underline{4 \times\ \ 7 =\ \ 28} \\
888
\end{array}
$$

Teacher: I saw that a lot of people recorded like Selina did. Some of you thought of some quicker ways to record your multiplication, and some of you asked me to show you some quicker ways when you saw other people using them. Here are some other ways to record the math that you are doing when you multiply. If you can keep track in your head what parts you have multiplied together, then you can just write the partial products, without writing the pairs of factors for each one, like this:

$$
\begin{array}{r}
37 \\
\underline{\times\, 24} \\
600 \\
140 \\
120 \\
\underline{28} \\
888
\end{array}
$$

You can find two partial products by using what you know about multiplying by a one-digit number. You can multiply 20×37 and record that partial product, then multiply 4×37 and record that partial product. Then add them together. [See fig. 2.10.]

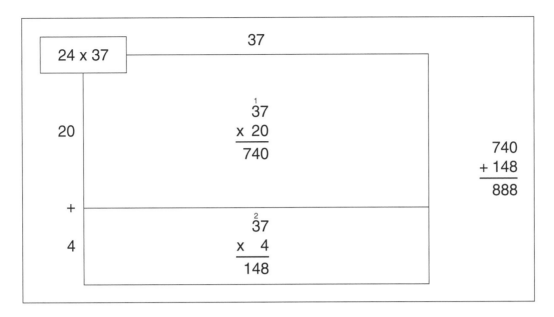

Fig. 2.10. Using partial products to solve 37 × 24

As seen in this example, students can drop steps from the full expanded notation method as they become more familiar with it, but a few may need to continue to use an expanded method as they work to develop fluency in using multidigit multiplication. Although recording all partial products may not be as efficient as using the current common method that collapses the recording into two partial products, as discussed in the next section, the various methods that involve recording different combinations of partial products are meaningful and generalizable methods that continue to build students' understanding of place value, decomposition of numbers, and multidigit multiplication.

Figure 2.11 illustrates various partial product representations for multiplication with three-digit numbers. Note that in this representation, the "regrouping" digits have been recorded in the appropriate place, directly above the sum, rather than at the top of the long column, to better keep track of them. Allowing students to make choices about which mathematically correct symbolic method of recording works best for them at any given time will allow them to solidify and apply the connections they have made among a variety of related multiplicative concepts and in turn will deepen their understanding of the mathematics involved in the standard algorithmic process for multidigit multiplication.

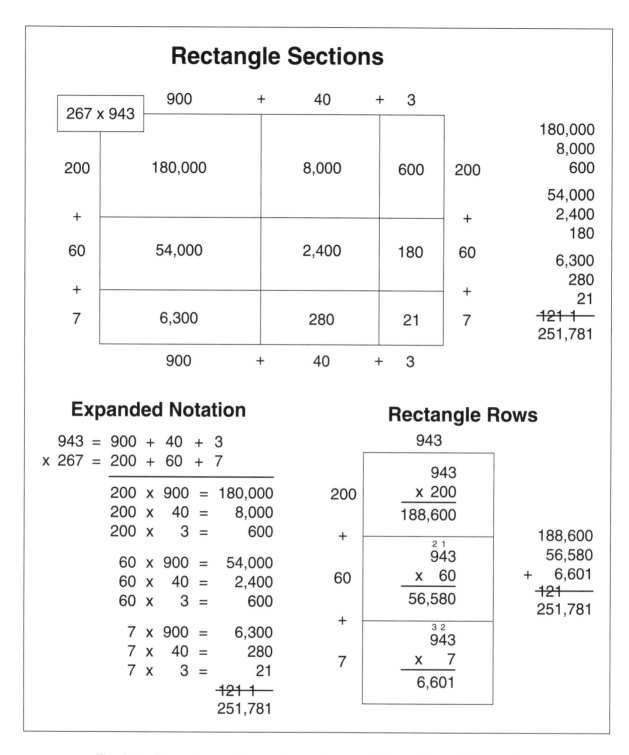

Fig. 2.11. Recording partial products when multiplying three-digit numbers

The collapsed method for recording multidigit multiplication

When discussing the steps of the collapsed method for recording the standard algorithmic approach for multidigit multiplication, the use of mathematically accurate language is essential to help students assign the appropriate value to each digit in the problem. Consistently using correct place-value language will, in itself, help correct many errors that students make with the standard algorithmic approach to multiplication, particularly with respect to writing numbers in the wrong places.

Figure 2.12 shows the steps for solving a two-digit-by-two-digit multiplication problem with the collapsed method of recording, an efficient but difficult-to-interpret symbolic representation. The use of correct and mathematically accurate language is important when discussing this approach with students. For example, in step 2 in figure 2.12, students must realize that they are multiplying by 20 and should record the resulting product appropriately by writing a 0 in the ones place and the 4 in the tens place. The very common error of writing 740 as 74 is made when students think they are multiplying 2×37 instead of 20×37. Always being cognizant of the value of each digit in the numbers being multiplied will help students avoid mistakes of this type.

Step 1	Step 1 in multiplying 24×37
Multiply by the ones. Regroup as necessary. [$(4 \times 37) = 148.$]	$\begin{array}{r} {}^{2} \\ 37 \\ \times\ 24 \\ \hline 148 \end{array}$
Step 2 Place a zero in the ones place of the next partial product because you are multiplying by tens. Multiply by the tens digit. Regroup as necessary. [$(20 \times 37) = 740.$]	Step 2 in multiplying 24×37 $\begin{array}{r} {}^{1} \\ {}^{2} \\ 37 \\ \times\ 24 \\ \hline 148 \\ 740 \\ \hline \end{array}$
Step 3 Add the partial products together. [$(4 \times 37) + (20 \times 37) =$ $148 + 740 = 888.$]	$\begin{array}{r} {}^{1} \\ {}^{2} \\ 37 \\ \times\ 24 \\ \hline 148 \\ 740 \\ \hline 888 \end{array}$

Fig. 2.12. Steps in the collapsed method for recording multidigit multiplication

Estimation and fluency in multiplication

One aspect of fluency in whole-number multiplication is the ability to use estimation to approximate products and to determine the reasonableness of exact results. Encouraging students to use estimation to determine whether an answer is reasonable will help them catch errors they might make because of digit misalignment or place-value mistakes. Students again connect a variety of different skills to accomplish this task, including rounding, patterns in powers of 10, and basic multiplication facts. For example, if students are given the problem 425 × 8, they can use their understanding of place value and number sense to know that 425 rounded to the nearest 100 is 400. This understanding allows students to use their knowledge of multiplying by powers of 10 to find that 400 × 8 = 3200. As students progress toward using more sophisticated multiplication algorithms, they need to be able to mentally calculate simple products (e.g., the extended facts that involve the patterns with zeros, such as 60 × 7 and 60 × 70) for both estimates and exact answers. This ability allows students to be accurate in their calculations as well as use estimation to check their answers for reasonableness.

Strengthening understanding of multiplication through problem solving

Using multiplication to solve problems can help students better understand the operation and its applications. Comparison-type problems that involve the idea of "scaling" lay the groundwork for general application of multiplication to fractions and decimals. Problems that involve counting combinations of elements of different sets can also enhance students' understanding of multiplication.

Using multiplication to solve comparison (scalar) problems

Students can use problem solving to extend their understanding of basic multiplication and division facts to multiplicative comparison problems, which most students find more difficult to interpret than joining equal groups. In a multiplicative comparison (or scalar) situation, one amount is expressed as a certain number of times as much as another amount. The scalar interpretation of multiplication is an important application for students to encounter and begin to understand, as it can build depth of understanding when learning multiplication by a fraction. In solving these problems, students' emerging understanding of the relationship between multiplication and division and fractions comes into play.

For example, consider this problem: "Janet picked 6 times as many apples as her little brother, Sean, picked. Sean picked 8 apples. How many apples did Janet pick?" Students can use their understanding of multiplication as well as their knowledge of basic facts to solve problems of this type. By making simple drawings of bars that show the scalar relationship between the two amounts as shown in figure 2.13, in which Janet's amount is six times Sean's amount, students can connect this representation with their prior understanding of multiplication as joining equal amounts. To solve this problem, students see that Janet has 6 × 8 = 48 apples.

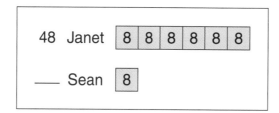

Fig. 2.13. Modeling a multiplicative comparison problem

Students can use this same type of multiplicative comparison, or scalar, representation to solve division, or unknown-factor, problems. For example, "Janet picked 6 times as many apples as her little brother, Sean, picked. Janet picked 48 apples. How many apples did Sean pick?" To solve this problem, students can draw the same diagram as in figure 2.13, but without knowing what number goes into the equal parts. They must think, "What number, when multiplied by 6, gives a total of 48, or 6 × ? = 48. Students who can automatically recall their multiplication facts will quickly determine that the answer is 8. Students who have not yet developed automatic recall for all facts can still address problems of this type by looking for the product of 48 in a multiplication chart or by counting by sixes.

Using multiplication to solve combination problems

Students find combination problems especially challenging because the multiplicative nature of the situation is not as apparent. Relating these situations to familiar models for multiplication—such as arrays, areas, and equal groups—will help students realize that these situations are also multiplicative. Consider this example: "Jill has 4 shirts and 3 pairs of pants in her closet that all go together. How many different combinations of 1 shirt and 1 pair of pants can Jill make?" Illustrating the problem using familiar multiplication models, such as the array shown in figure 2.14, helps students understand that the problem is a multiplication situation. In this problem, each of the 4 shirts represents a group of 3 pants that it could be matched with, so 4 groups of 3 are possible. Alternatively, each of the 3 pairs of pants represents a group of 4 shirts that it could be matched with. Students need to multiply 4 × 3 to get the total number of outfit combinations.

	3 Types of Pants		
	Jeans	**Tan Pants**	**Black Pants**
Red shirt	Red shirt Jeans	Red shirt Tan pants	Red shirt Black pants
Blue shirt	Blue shirt Jeans	Blue shirt Tan pants	Blue shirt Black pants
Green shirt	Green shirt Jeans	Green shirt Tan pants	Green shirt Black pants
Yellow shirt	Yellow shirt Jeans	Yellow shirt Tan pants	Yellow shirt Black pants

(4 Colors of Shirts — row label on left side)

4 shirts × 3 pants = 3 pants × 4 shirts = 12 different combinations.

Fig. 2.14. A combination problem solved with multiplication

Students can fill in columns and rows inside the chart in figure 2.14 and then see that the array model has 4 rows, 1 for each color of shirt, and 3 columns, 1 for each type of pants. This representation is an array; so by multiplying the number of rows by the number of columns, students find the total number of combinations. Connecting the new and unfamiliar multiplication situation with a more familiar multiplication model emphasizes the multiplicative nature of combination problems.

Using problem solving to learn about remainders

In grade 3, students learned about two basic equal-groups division situations:

- "How many in each group?" or partitive, division situations, and

- "How many groups?" or measurement, division situations.

In partitive division problems, the total and the number of groups are given and students need to find the number in each group. In measurement division problems, the total and the number in each group are given and students need to find the number of groups.

Using problems that build on this understanding of division, but do not "come out even" when doing the division, will help students in grade 4 use their knowledge of division facts to begin their work with remainders. In early explorations of division with remainders, students can use familiar division models to solve non–basic fact division equations, such as $35 \div 8 =$ __. As shown in figure 2.15, students observe that if they divide 35 into 8 groups, the result is 4 objects in each group with 3 objects left over. Similarly, if they divide 35 into groups of 8 objects, the result is 4 groups with 3 objects left over.

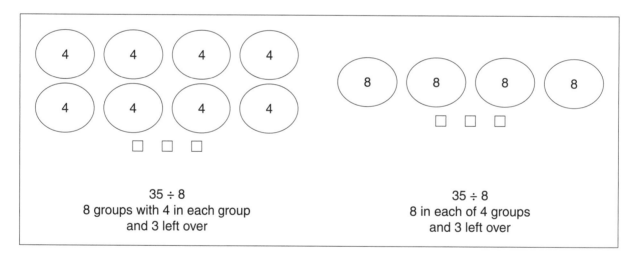

Fig. 2.15. Modeling division with remainders

After understanding the meaning of remainder depicted in figure 2.15, students need to be encouraged to use their understanding of division's relationship to multiplication as "finding an unknown factor" to develop a sense of "closest basic fact under" concept. In the example $35 \div 8 =$ __, students move from modeling to thinking of multiples of 8 that are close to 35. For example, they might think of $4 \times 8 = 32$ and $5 \times 8 = 40$. Since 40 is greater than 35, students realize that when 35 objects are divided equally among 8 groups, the largest whole number of objects that can be put in each group is 4, and 3 objects are left over. Similarly, when 35 objects are divided into groups of 8, the largest whole number of groups of 8 that can be made is 4, and 3 objects are left over. Consequently, $4 \times 8 = 32$ is the "closest basic fact" of 8 "under" 35. Through the meaningful application of this concept coupled with their understanding of division, students determine that 35 ÷ 8 = 4 R3. The models in figure 2.15 illustrate that 35 ÷ 8 = 4 R3 can also be written 8 × 4 + 3 = 35 because it illustrates both that 8 groups of 4 plus 3 more is equal to 35 and that 4 groups of 8 plus 3 more is 35. Thus, again, the relationship between multiplication and division is reinforced. Students can use this relationship to check their answers to division problems. The successful assimilation of these concepts forms the foundation students will need to move on to multidigit division in grade 5.

Strengthening Fluency in Multiplication through Connections

Facilitating connections between multiplication and other topics in mathematics helps strengthen students' fluency in both multiplication and the connected ideas. The relationship between powers of 10 and multiplication previously addressed provides an opportunity for students to connect multiplication and algebraic reasoning. Through identifying, describing, and extending numeric patterns in powers of 10 and the products associated with them, students can begin to develop an understanding of algebraic functions. Figure 2.16 shows a function table with the rule "multiply a number by 30." Students can use their understanding of multiplication and their ability to extend and complete algebraic patterns to apply this rule to find the missing outputs and complete the table.

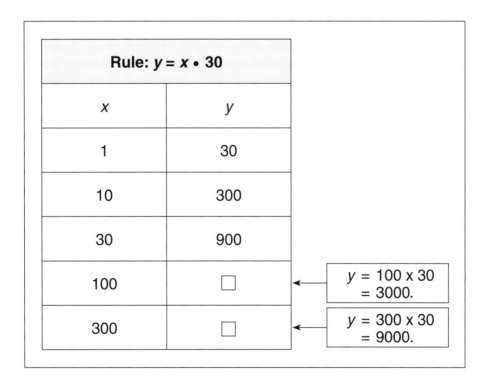

Fig. 2.16. Connecting multiplication and algebraic reasoning in a function table

Another connection alluded to previously occurs with multiplicative comparison problems. Multiplicative comparison problems can also lead to a deeper understanding of the connections among multiplication, division, and fractions. Recall the previous problem, "Janet picked 6 times as many apples as her little brother, Sean, picked. Janet picked 48 apples. How many apples did Sean pick?" In that problem, students can use the unknown-factor multiplication fact 6 × ? = 48 to solve the problem.

However, the question can be asked in two ways to connect with multiplication with fractions. If Janet picked 6 times as many apples as Sean, then we also know that Sean picked 1/6 as many apples as Janet. Although not standard in English, we could also say that Sean picked 1/6 *times* as many apples as Janet. Thus, students can use 1/6 of 48 to find the answer. As students study the problem further, they can begin to understand how the problem also illustrates the connection between fractions and division. Students can build the connection that to find 1/6 of a number, they must divide the number into 6 equal parts. Thus, finding 1/6 of a number is the same as dividing the number by 6. The opportunities to develop rich mathematical understanding of connections between concepts presented in problems of this type are enhanced by students' having a firm understanding of the meaning of multiplication and the ability to recall the multiplication facts fairly quickly. Without these underpinnings, students have to work much harder to make these connections as they arise.

Connections in Later Grades

In grade 4, students are asked to apply their knowledge of multiplying with powers of 10 to solve more complicated division problems. Knowing and understanding the relationship of multiplication and division and the connections among products that are related by 10, 100, or 1000 are crucial to understanding and implementing the mental methods and multidigit division strategies that students will encounter in grade 5. For example, a student who understands the related products illustrated in figure 2.5 and understands division as "finding an unknown factor" will recognize the relationships among the following division problems:

$$6 \div 3 = 2,$$
$$60 \div 3 = 20,$$
$$600 \div 3 = 200$$

and

$$6 \div 2 = 3,$$
$$60 \div 20 = 3,$$
$$600 \div 200 = 3.$$

This understanding will be valuable in grade 5 when students progress from multiplying multidigit numbers to using the division algorithm to divide multidigit numbers. If students have developed the necessary understanding of, and fluency with, multiplication in grade 4, then they will more easily make the connections necessary in grade 5 to learn and meaningfully apply the standard algorithmic procedure for division.

Measuring Depth of Understanding

Figure 2.17 presents five ways to represent the product 37 × 24: rectangle sections, rectangle rows, expanded notation, and two shortcuts. What do students need to know about numbers and operations to be able to interpret and create each of these representations? What criteria will you use to evaluate students' progress in developing fluency with multidigit multiplication?

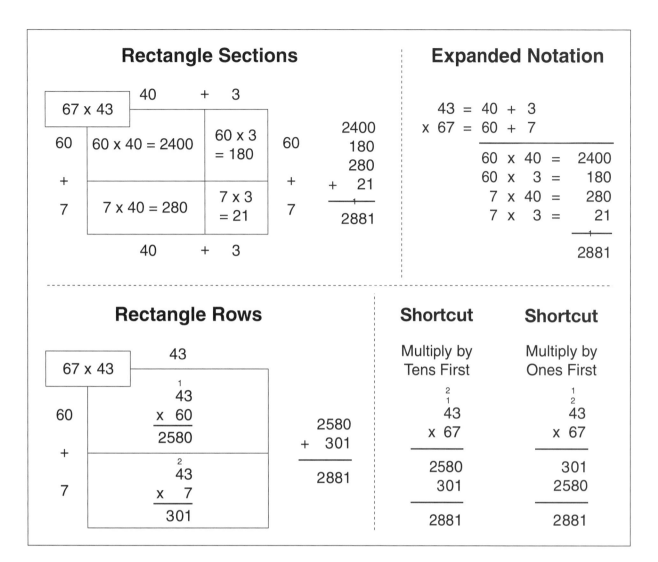

Fig. 2.17. Five ways to represent the product 37 × 24

3 Focusing on Fractions and Decimals

In grade 4, students are introduced to decimals. The focus in this grade is on understanding relationships between fractions and decimals. Like fractions, numbers with decimal places to the right of the ones place can be used to name values that are between whole numbers. To visualize fraction-decimal relationships, students use fraction models with which they are familiar, especially area models and the number line. An emphasis is placed on the understanding that decimal notation is an extension to the right of the ones place of the base-ten system. Students use their understanding of relationships between fractions and decimals as well as decimal place value to visualize, represent, and communicate about decimals.

Instructional Progression for Connecting Fractions and Decimals

The focus on fluency with fractions and decimals in grade 4 is supported by a progression of related mathematical ideas before and after grade 4, as shown in table 3.1. To give perspective to the grade 4 work, we first discuss some of the important ideas that students focused on in grade 3 that prepared them for expanded work with fractions and new work with decimals in grade 4. At the end of the detailed discussion of this grade 4 focal point, we present examples of how students will use their fraction and decimal understandings and skills in later grades. For more detailed discussions of the "before" and "after" parts of the instructional progression, please see the appropriate grade-level books, that is, *Focus in Grade 3* (NCTM 2009) and *Focus in Grade 5* (NCTM 2009).

Table 3.1 represents an instructional progression for the understanding of fractions and decimals in grades 3 through 5.

Early Foundations of Fractions

In grade 3, students begin their focus on fractions. In the study of fractions, a variety of concrete and pictorial experiences have students represent a fraction as a part of a whole in an area model, as a part of a set, and as a distance designated by a point on the number line (a type of linear model). Students begin to build understanding of the idea that a fraction is a relationship of two numbers—the denominator, which names the parts on the basis of how many equal parts are in the whole, and the numerator, which tells the number of equal parts being considered.

To develop an understanding of a fraction as part of a whole, students can use area models. For example, the area models in figure 3.1 show 3 one-fourths, or 3/4.

Table 3.1

Grade 4: Focusing on Fractions and Decimals

Instructional Progression for Developing Understanding in Grades 3–5

Grade 3	Grade 4	Grade 5
Students use unit fractions (1/*n*) to represent equal divisions of a whole. Students create nonunit fractions by joining unit fractions (e.g. 2/3 is the same as 1/3 + 1/3) and build a whole (1) by joining "*n*" of the unit fraction (1/*n*). Students judge the size of a fractional part by relating it to the size of the whole. Students compare unit fractions of the same-sized whole by observing that the larger the denominator, the smaller the amount represented by the unit fraction. Students use fractions to represent numbers that are equal to, less than, or greater than 1. Students compare and order fractions by using models, benchmark fractions, common numerators, and common denominators. Students use models, including the number line, to identify equivalent fractions. Students use fractional parts of units to measure length. **	Students analyze techniques that involve multiplication and division to generate equivalent fractions.** Students identify equivalent symbolic representations of improper fractions and mixed numbers. Students use decimal notation as an extension of the base-ten system to the right of the ones place. Students use their understanding of fractions and place value to read and write decimals that are greater than 1 or between 0 and 1. Students connect equivalent fractions and decimals by comparing models with symbols and using equivalent symbols to describe the same point on a number line. Students use place-value notation and equivalent fractions to identify equivalent decimals. Students use place-value notation and understanding of fractions to compare and order decimals.	Students apply their understanding of fractions and fraction models to add and subtract fractions with like and unlike denominators. Students apply their understanding of decimal models, place value, and properties to add and subtract decimals. Students work toward fluency in adding and subtracting fractions and decimals. Students make reasonable estimates of fraction and decimal sums and differences. Students add and subtract fractions and decimals to solve problems, including problems involving measurement.

*   Appears in Grade 3 Connections to the Focal Points.

**   Appears in Grade 4 Connections to the Focal Points.

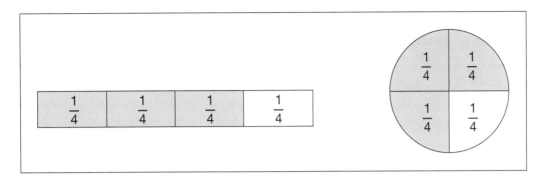

Fig. 3.1. Using area models to show 3/4

Students also use linear models, such as fraction strips, fraction bars, and the number line, to represent a fraction as a part of a whole. For example, the fraction-bar model in figure 3.2 shows 3/8.

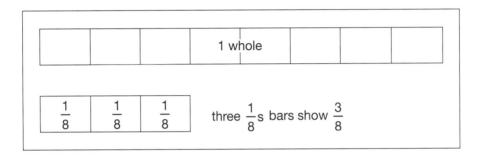

Fig. 3.2. Using fraction bars to show 3/8

Students can also illustrate the same relationship between a fraction (e.g., 3/8) and the unit (1) by using a point on the number line, as in figure 3.3.

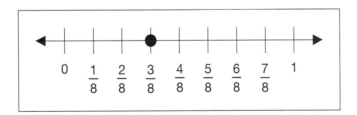

Fig. 3.3. Using the number line to represent 3/8

To show that a fraction can identify a part of a whole set, students can use set models like the model shown in figure 3.4.

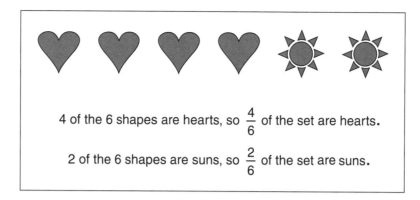

4 of the 6 shapes are hearts, so $\frac{4}{6}$ of the set are hearts.

2 of the 6 shapes are suns, so $\frac{2}{6}$ of the set are suns.

Fig. 3.4. Representing a fraction as a part of a set

Students can use these same types of representations to learn about fractions equal to, or greater than, 1. Students use models like the one shown in figure 3.5 to show the relationship between improper fractions (fractions in which the numerator is equal to, or greater than, the denominator) and whole numbers or mixed numbers. Students can see that 7 thirds are shaded, so the model shows 7/3. They also see that 2 wholes and 1/3 of another whole are shaded, so the model shows $2\frac{1}{3}$. From this model, students learn that $7/3 = 2\frac{1}{3}$. As students work with these types of models, they may also notice that some improper fractions are equivalent to whole numbers rather than mixed numbers. For example, in figure 3.5, they can also see that 6/3 = 2.

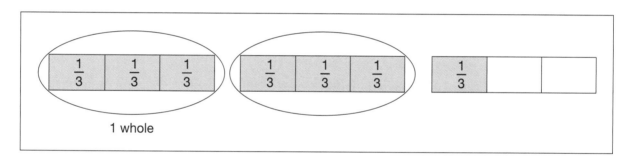

Fig. 3.5. Using a model to establish the equivalence between $7/3$ and $2\frac{1}{3}$

In grade 3, students have opportunities to see that different fractions are equivalent if they represent the same amount in relation to the whole. Students can use area and linear models as shown in figure 3.6 to visualize equivalent fractions. The models show that 1/3 = 2/6 = 3/9 and that 2/3 = 4/6 = 6/9 = 8/12.

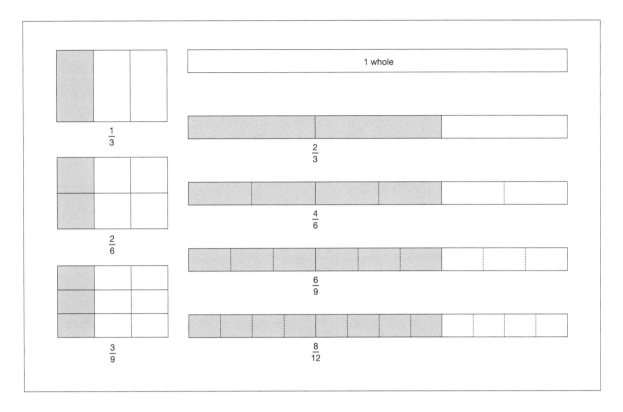

Fig. 3.6. Area and linear models representing equivalent fractions

Models such as the ones in figure 3.6 also emphasize the relationship between the number of parts in the whole and the size of each part. Students can use these models to internalize the ideas that the more parts into which a whole is divided, the smaller the size of each part, and the more parts that are needed to form the same portion of the whole. These important relationships foster the understanding that students will call on as they learn to use multiplication and division to find equivalent fractions in grade 4, as well as when they add and subtract fractions with unlike denominators in grade 5.

In grade 3, students are also asked to compare two fractions that are not equal. To compare fractions that have the same denominator, students can use their understanding that two fractions with the same denominator indicate a whole or wholes that have been divided into the same number of equal-sized parts, so the fraction with the larger numerator has the larger number of equal parts and is the larger fraction. For example, the number-line model in figure 3.7 clearly shows that 5/8 is larger than 3/8.

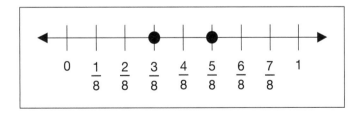

Fig. 3.7. Number-line representation of the principle that if the denominators are the same, the fraction with the larger numerator is the larger fraction

To compare fractions that have the same numerator, students can draw on the understanding of the principle of the inverse relationship between the number of equal parts in a whole and the size of the parts. For example, as the models for 3/8 and 3/10 presented in figure 3.8 illustrate, in relation to the same whole, tenths are smaller than eighths, so 3/10 is smaller than 3/8.

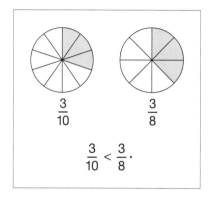

Fig. 3.8. Pictorial representation of the principle that if the numerators are the same, the fraction with the larger denominator is the smaller fraction

Students can also use fractional number sense to compare fractions by considering how they relate to benchmark numbers, such as 0, 1/2, or 1. For example, if a student knows that one fraction is less than 1/2 and another fraction is greater than 1/2, then the student can determine that the first fraction is less than the second fraction. Students can also compare fractions with 1. For example, to compare 4/5 and 7/8, students understand that if 4/5 is 1/5 away from 1 whereas 7/8 is 1/8 away from 1, and that 1/8 is less than 1/5, then 7/8 is closer to 1 than 4/5 is. So 7/8 > 4/5.

In grade 3, students can also use the fractional number sense they have developed to order fractions. For example, students might order 2/5, 1/5, and 5/7 by reasoning that if 2/5 is less than 1/2 whereas 5/7 is greater than 1/2, and that 1/5 is less than 2/5, then the order of the numbers is 1/5, 2/5, 5/7.

In grade 4, students will augment these strategies for comparing and ordering fractions by learning how to use multiplication and division to write equivalent fractions with the same denominator to compare fractions. For further details on the grade 3 focal point Focusing on Fractions, refer to *Focus in Grade 3* (NCTM 2009).

Connecting Fractions and Decimals

Extending fraction concepts

In grade 4, students continue to connect the concrete and pictorial representations used in grade 3 with symbolic representations to extend fraction concepts. Finding patterns in equivalent fractions is one example of this extension. In grade 4, students begin to use multiplication and division to identify the equivalent fractions that they recognized with models in grade 3.

In grade 4, students are led to the generalization that to find a fraction equivalent to another fraction, they can multiply or divide the numerator and denominator by the same number. The fraction strip becomes a powerful representation through which students can gain an understanding of this mathematical relationship. For example, as shown in figure 3.9, students can fold a fraction strip into thirds and shade 2 of the thirds to show 2/3. Then they can fold the strip again to divide each third in half. As students interpret the fraction strip, they can see that their strip shows sixths and that what was 2 thirds is now

4 sixths, or 2/3 = 4/6. Students begin to understand, then, the fundamental principle of using multiplication to find fractions. When they folded each third in half, they multiplied the number of parts in the whole, that is, the denominator, 3, by 2. When they counted the parts, 2 times as many parts were shaded, which is the same as multiplying the numerator, 2, by 2. As students' understanding matures, they can use the models to internalize the crucial relationship between the size of the parts and the number of parts in the whole that they developed in grade 3. They begin to understand that 2/3 and 4/6 represent the same amount of the strip because, although the whole has 2 times as many parts in 4/6 than it does in 2/3, the parts are half as big. So multiplying the numerator and denominator by 2 results in an equivalent fraction that names the same part of the whole. Students can apply the same understanding to multiply the numerator and denominator by 3 to find that 2/3 = 6/9, and multiply the numerator and denominator by 4 to find that 2/3 = 8/12.

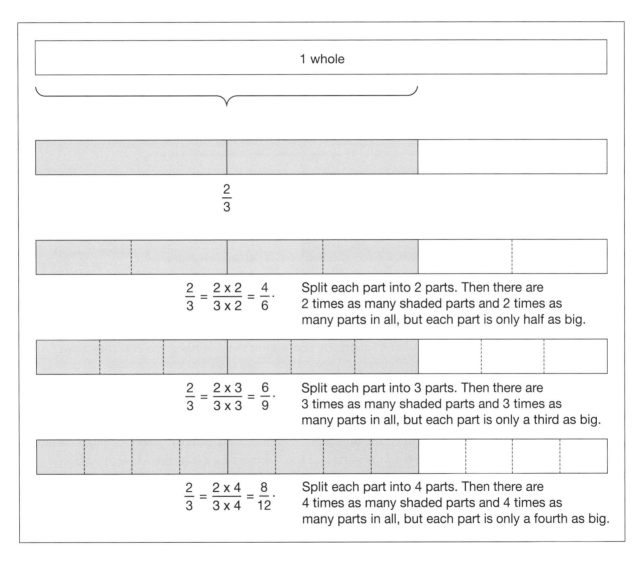

Fig. 3.9. Linear model illustrating why forming equivalent fractions by splitting parts is the same as multiplying the total number of parts and the number of shaded parts by the same number

An interesting relationship to note in figure 3.9 is that students physically *divide* the whole fraction bar, yet numerically they *multiply* the numerator and denominator of 2/3. As students interpret a variety of fraction models such as the ones shown in figure 3.9, they are given opportunities to observe that when the denominator and numerator of a fraction are each multiplied by a positive number, the resulting fraction refers to more parts but each part is a smaller fraction of a whole.

By reversing the process shown in figure 3.9 and joining the parts of a whole, students can also use a fraction strip to demonstrate why dividing the numerator and denominator of a fraction by the same number results in an equivalent fraction. As shown in figure 3.10, the whole is divided into 15 equal parts and 10 of them are shaded to model 10/15. Students can join groups of 5 parts. The result is a whole that is divided into 3 equal groups. As students interpret the model, they can see that the strip now shows thirds and that what was 10 fifteenths is now 2 thirds, so 10/15 = 2/3.

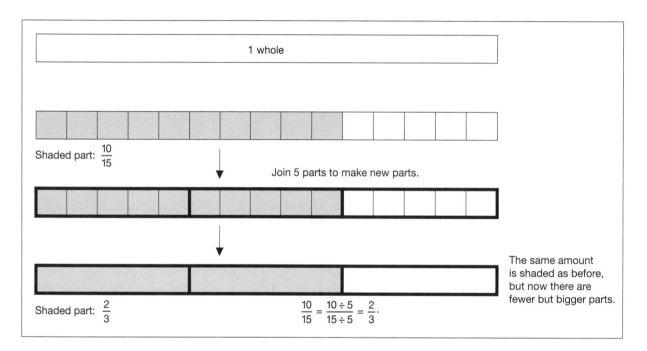

Fig. 3.10. Linear model illustrating how forming equivalent fractions by joining original parts into larger parts is related to forming equivalent fractions by separating the original parts into smaller parts

Students begin to understand, then, the fundamental principle of using division of both the numerator and denominator to find equivalent fractions. When they joined groups of 5 parts, they divided the number of parts in the whole, that is, the denominator, 15, by 5. When they counted the parts, 2 parts were shaded, which illustrated that they divided the numerator, 10, by 5. This pattern further emphasizes the important relationship between the size of the parts and the number of parts in the whole. The fractions 10/15 and 2/3 represent the same amount of the strip because, although the whole is partitioned into one-fifth as many parts in 2/3 as in 10/15, the parts are 5 times larger. So dividing each of the numerator and denominator of 10/15 by 5 results in an equivalent fraction.

In figure 3.9, the number of parts was multiplied by a number resulting in more parts. In figure 3.10, the number of parts was divided by a number resulting in fewer parts. Through an abundance of concrete and pictorial experiences with separating and joining groups to make related representations of equal fractional amounts, students experience that multiplying or dividing the numerator and denominator by the same number results in equivalent fractions.

Students can use a multiplication table to apply the multiplicative patterns in equivalent fractions. For example, in the hundreds chart in figure 3.11, students can look from left to right across the 2 row for numerators and across the 5 row for denominators to see that 2/5 = 4/10 = 6/15 = 8/20 = 10/25, and so on. They can also look from right to left across the 4 row for numerators and the 9 row for denominators to see that 4/5 = 40/90 = 36/81 = 32/72 = 28/63 = 24/54, and so on. As students' understanding of equivalent fractions matures, they can be led to observe that this pattern occurs because the numbers in each row increase by a factor of 2 from column 1 to column 2, by a factor of 3 from column 1 to column 3, by a factor of 4 from column 1 to column 4, and so on, as indicated by the equations in figure 3.11.

x	1	2	3	4	5	6	7	8	9	10
1	1	2	3	4	5	6	7	8	9	10
2	2	4	6	8	10	12	14	16	18	20
3	3	6	9	12	15	18	21	24	27	30
4	4	8	12	16	20	24	28	32	36	40
5	5	10	15	20	25	30	35	40	45	50
6	6	12	18	24	30	36	42	48	54	60
7	7	14	21	28	35	42	49	56	63	70
8	8	16	24	32	40	48	56	64	72	80
9	9	18	27	36	45	54	63	72	81	90
10	10	20	30	40	50	60	70	80	90	100

$$\overset{\times 2}{\underset{\times 2}{\frac{2}{5} = \frac{4}{10}}} \quad \overset{\times 3}{\underset{\times 3}{\frac{2}{5} = \frac{6}{15}}} \quad \overset{\times 4}{\underset{\times 4}{\frac{2}{5} = \frac{8}{20}}} \quad \overset{\times 5}{\underset{\times 5}{\frac{2}{5} = \frac{10}{25}}} \quad \overset{\times 6}{\underset{\times 6}{\frac{2}{5} = \frac{12}{30}}}$$

$$\overset{\div 10}{\underset{\div 10}{\frac{40}{90} = \frac{4}{9}}} \quad \overset{\div 9}{\underset{\div 9}{\frac{36}{81} = \frac{4}{9}}} \quad \overset{\div 8}{\underset{\div 8}{\frac{32}{72} = \frac{4}{9}}} \quad \overset{\div 7}{\underset{\div 7}{\frac{28}{63} = \frac{4}{9}}} \quad \overset{\div 6}{\underset{\div 6}{\frac{24}{54} = \frac{4}{9}}}$$

Fig 3.11. Equivalent fractions in the multiplication table

The ability to symbolically calculate equivalent fractions is essential to students' further study of fractions. They can use this method when they compare fractions. For example, they may have difficulty using benchmarks or fractional number sense to compare such fractions as 4/7 and 3/5. So to compare such fractions without models, students can find equivalent fractions with the same denominators. They can use the process described above to multiply the numerator and denominator in 4/7 by 5 to find that 4/7 =

20/35 and to multiply the numerator and denominator in 3/5 by 7 to find that 3/5 = 21/35. Once the fractions are written with like denominators, students can compare them by comparing numerators: 20/35 < 21/35, so 4/7 < 3/5. In grade 5, students will use equivalent fractions with like denominators to add and subtract any pair of fractions.

The relationship between improper fractions and mixed numbers

In grade 4, students work on transitioning from the concrete and pictorial to the symbolic as they extend their understanding of relationships between improper fractions and mixed numbers. Students formalize this relationship when they learn how to write an improper fraction as a mixed number and a mixed number as an improper fraction without the use of the models that formed the basis for their work in grade 3. In grade 3, students observed that numbers greater than 1 that are not whole numbers could be written as equivalent improper fractions and mixed numbers. For example, the model in 3.12 shows 14/3 because 14 thirds are shaded; as well as shows $4\frac{2}{3}$ because 4 wholes and $\frac{2}{3}$ of another whole are shaded.

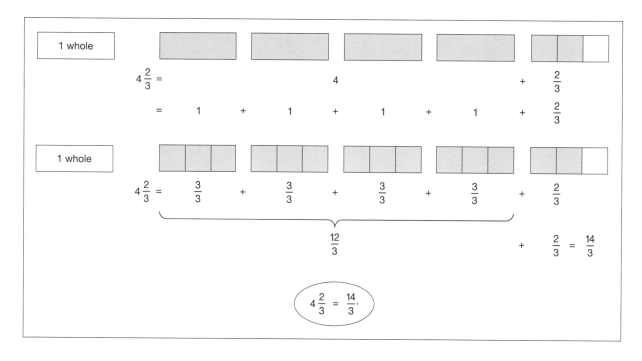

Fig. 3.12. Model showing the relationship between improper fractions and mixed numbers

In grade 4, students progress in their understanding of the relationship between equivalent forms of the same fraction, such as $^{14}/_3$ and $4^2/_3$. As illustrated in figure 3.13, students can use the model of $4^2/_3$ to write an equivalent improper fraction. Students can see that 1 whole equals 3/3, so for every whole in the model, they need 3 thirds. So to write $4^2/_3$ as an improper fraction, they can join 4 groups of 3 thirds (or 4 × 3 = 12 thirds) and add the additional 2 thirds to make 14 thirds in all. Through these concrete and pictorial experiences, students begin to generalize that to change a mixed number to an improper fraction, they multiply the number of parts in the whole (or the denominator of the fraction part of the mixed number) by the number of wholes (or the whole-number part of the mixed number) and add the number of parts represented by the numerator in the mixed number. The result is the number of parts in the improper fraction (or the numerator of the improper fraction). The number of parts in the whole does not change, so the denominator of the improper fraction is the same.

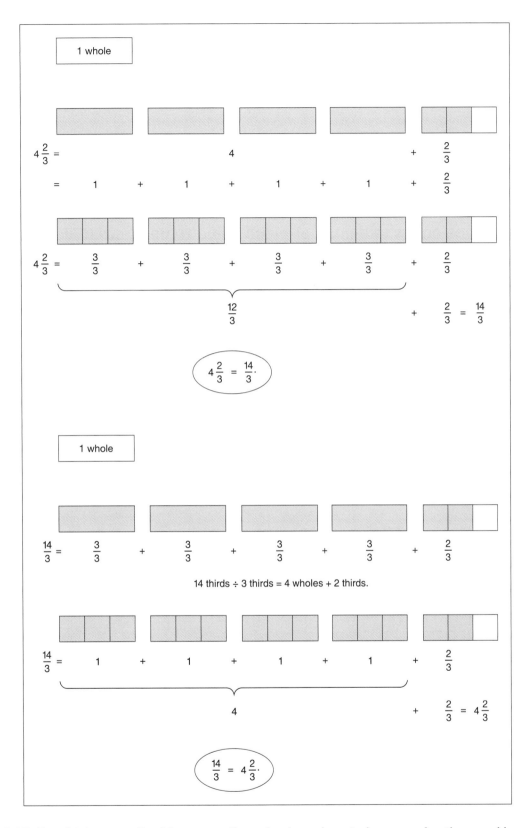

Fig. 3.13. Developing a method for converting mixed numbers to improper fractions and improper fractions to mixed numbers

Conversely, students can use the model of 14/3 to write an equivalent mixed number. They know that each whole is composed of 3 thirds, so they can use reasoning and their division facts to find the number of 3 thirds in 14 thirds by dividing 14 by 3. They can see from their model that 14 thirds has 4 groups of 3 thirds with 2 thirds left over. Thus, they know that 14/3 = 4 wholes + 2 thirds, or $4\frac{2}{3}$. Through a variety of concrete and pictorial experiences, students learn to generalize that to write a mixed number as an equivalent improper fraction, they divide the numerator of the improper fraction (number of fractional parts) by the denominator of the improper fraction (the number of parts in a whole) to find the number of wholes and write that number as the whole-number part of the mixed number; the remainder of that division (the number of fractional parts left over) is the numerator of the fraction part of the mixed number.

Using fractions and whole-number place value to understand decimals

In grade 4, students use place value and decimal notation to represent fractional amounts. A student's understanding of decimal notation requires the use of basic meanings of fractions with denominators of 10, 100, and 1000, as well as the idea that the same fractional amount can be represented by many equivalent symbols and the understanding of the relationships between the positions in place-value notation.

In grades 2 and 3, students are exposed to the base-ten number system for whole-number place values through thousands. Because decimal place value is an extension of whole-number place value, these whole-number experiences help form the foundation for students' work with decimals in grade 4. Students use place-value charts, as shown in figure 3.14, to distinguish the place values from the ones place through the thousands place.

thousands	hundreds	tens	ones
2	7	3	8

thousands	hundreds	tens	ones
3	8	7	2

Fig. 3.14. Place-value chart showing whole-number place-value positions

Students learn that strings of different arrangements of the ten digits 0, 1, 2, 3, 4, 5, 6, 7, 8, and 9 are written together to represent different numbers. The value of each digit in a number depends on its position, or place, in the number. For example, in figure 3.12, in the number 2738, the digit 3 is in the tens place, so it has a value of 3 tens, or 30. In the number 3872, however, the digit 3 is in the thousands place; so in the number 3872, it has a value of 3 thousands, or 3000. The digit is the same, but its value in a number changes on the basis of its position in the number and the corresponding place's value. In the base-ten system, the value of each place is ten times the value of the place to the right. The *base-ten* system gets its name from the fact that it is *based* on powers of *10*. This relationship is illustrated in figure 3.15.

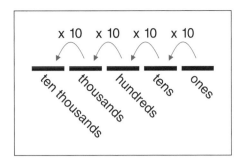

Fig. 3.15. Pictorial representation of the power-of-10 relationship in the place values of whole numbers

This process of multiplying a value by 10 to create a new, larger value that is recorded in the place to the left continues indefinitely. Students also learn that the first place to the left of the ones place, the tens place, has a value of 10×1. The second place to the left of the ones place, the hundreds place, has a value of 100×1, and so on for larger and larger whole-number place values. A firm understanding of this multiplicative relationship is vital to students' understanding in grade 4 of the symmetrical pattern created by the whole-number and decimal place values.

Students also can observe that when moving to the right across the places, each place has the value of the one before it divided by 10, as indicated in figure 3.16. Students use this pattern of dividing by 10 as they develop decimal place-value concepts by observing that this pattern continues to the right of the ones place indefinitely and results in the decimal place values. This process of dividing a value by 10 to create a new, lesser value that is recorded in the place to the right continues indefinitely, so the decimal place values continue to get infinitely smaller to the right just as the whole-number place values continue to get infinitely larger to the left.

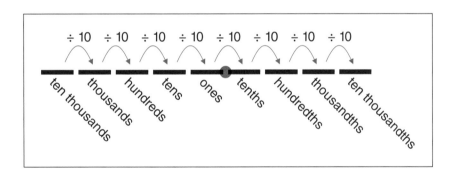

Fig. 3.16. Pictorial representation showing that each place's value is the one to the left of it divided by 10 (or 1/10 the value of the place to its left)

If a whole is divided by 10, each part is 1 tenth of the whole, so the value of the tenths place is 1/10 of the ones place. If 1 tenth is divided by 10, each part is 1 tenth of a tenth, so the hundredths place is 1/100 of the value of the ones place, and so on. Area models for decimals, such as the one in figure 3.17, can help students understand the meanings of fractional decimal places. Viewing the values of the places in this way allows students to assimilate their understanding of whole-number place value and fractions to develop the concept of decimal places and to understand the values that decimal numbers represent.

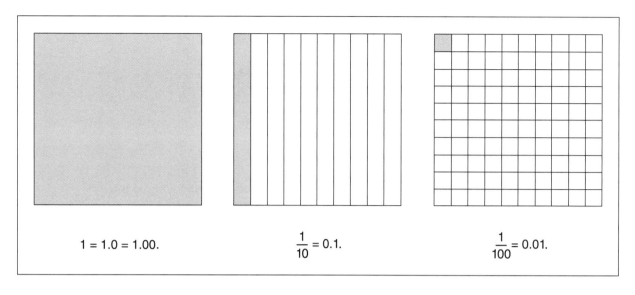

$$1 = 1.0 = 1.00. \qquad \frac{1}{10} = 0.1. \qquad \frac{1}{100} = 0.01.$$

Fig. 3.17. Area models that help students connect fractions and decimals

In grade 4, students use this pattern to expand their understanding of the base-ten number system as a way to represent such numbers as 14.1 and 3.95 and 284.007. In grade 3, students used whole-number place value to understand, read, and write whole numbers. They also encountered the idea of mixed numbers as they studied fractions. As students begin to study decimal numbers in grade 4, they learn that a marker, called a *decimal point,* is immediately to the right of the digit in the ones place and that the decimal numbers with digits on both the left and right side of the decimal point represent a mixed number with a whole-number part represented by the digits to the left of the decimal point and a fractional part represented by the digits to the right of the decimal point. If no nonzero digits appear to the left of the decimal point, then the decimal represents a number between 0 and 1.

Students can use their previous knowledge of whole-number place value coupled with their understanding of fractions to interpret these numerical representations. The vocabulary associated with decimal place values, such as tenths, hundredths, thousandths, and so on, is based on the fundamental relationship between decimal places and fractions. For example, when students learn to read the decimal 0.5 as 5 tenths, they hear the connection with 5/10, which is also read as 5 tenths, an equivalent form describing the same number, with the final goal being the realization that 5/10 = 0.5.

Decimals are an extension of the concepts developed in whole-number place value, so students can also use their understanding of whole-number place value to understand and explore decimals. For example, just as students used place-value charts to determine the value of each digit in a number such as 3421, they can use place-value charts, extended to the right to show the decimal places, to find the value of each digit in the number 534.21, as shown in figure 3.18.

hundreds	tens	ones	tenths	hundredths
5	3	4	2	1

Fig. 3.18. Example of the use of a place-value chart to show whole numbers and decimals

Note that the borders of the columns in the place-value chart in figure 3.18 are designed to show the decimal point as being closely related to the ones place—in other words, the symmetry of decimal place value is around the ones place including the decimal point, not just around the decimal point, because the decimal point by itself is not a place-value position. As students explore the symmetry that exists around the ones place (for example, one place to the left is tens, one place to the right is tenths), they can use their understanding of the whole-number place values to help them learn and understand the decimal place values.

As students learn about decimal place values in relation to whole-number place values, the correct symmetry of the places should be emphasized, as is illustrated in figure 3.19. In grade 3, students observed that the first place value to the left of the ones place, the tens, has a value of ten times one, or 10 × 1; the second place value to the left of the ones place, the hundreds, has a value of one hundred times one, or 100 × 1; and so on for larger and larger whole-number place values.

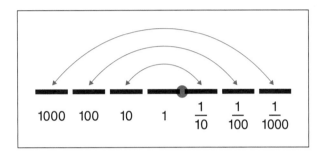

Fig. 3.19. The symmetry in value of place-value positions around the ones place

A similar pattern in the decimal place values creates a type of symmetry around the ones place. Students notice that the first place to the right of the ones place is the tenths place, which is one-tenth of one, or 1/10 × 1. The second place to the right of the ones place is the hundredths place, which is one hundredth of one, or 1/100 × 1, and so on for smaller and smaller decimal place values. Emphasizing this symmetry as the initial development of the framework for decimal place value will help prevent a common misconception that decimal symmetry is around the decimal point, a misconception that leads to difficulty in correctly identifying the denominators of decimal numbers.

Using fraction representations to interpret, visualize, and communicate about decimals

Once students are aware of the decimal system and the decimal form of numbers, they can use their accumulated knowledge of fractions to interpret, visualize, and communicate about decimals. To help students with this understanding, the models with which students are already familiar are used. Fractions that have a denominator of 10 naturally help students use their knowledge of fractions to understand decimals, because tenths is the first decimal place value to the right of the decimal point. In figure 3.20, an area model shows 3 tenths, or 3/10. Students learn that 3/10 can also be written 0.3, or as a decimal with a 3 in the tenths place.

Model	Fraction	Decimal
	$\dfrac{3}{10}$	0.3
	3 tenths	3 tenths

Fig. 3.20. Progression from model to fractional representation of tenths to decimal notation

Conversely, if they see the decimal 0.3 and know how to read the decimal as "3 tenths," they can relate that knowledge to the fraction 3/10, and because of their understanding of fractions, know that 3/10 is 3 out of 10 equal parts; so they correctly interpret 0.3 as 3 out of 10 equal parts. The progression from the model to the fraction representation to the decimal, as well as the reverse progression from decimal to fraction representation to model, work together to solidify students' understanding of the relationship between fractions and decimals.

Fractions that have a denominator of 100 also can help students in their transition from fraction concepts to decimal concepts. In figure 3.21, students see an area model of a whole divided into 100 parts with 23 parts shaded to represent 23/100. As they learn more about decimals, they learn that 23 hundredths can be written as the decimal 0.23. Thus, the fractional area model becomes a decimal grid that models 0.23.

Model	Fraction	Decimal
	$\dfrac{23}{100}$	0.23
	twenty-three hundredths	twenty-three hundredths

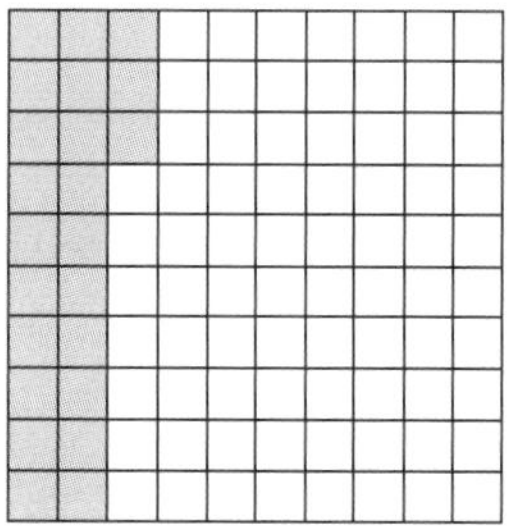

Fig 3.21. Connecting the area model, fraction notation, and decimal notation for a decimal number

Conversely, if they see the decimal 0.23 and know how to read the decimal as "23 hundredths," they can relate that knowledge to the fraction 23/100 and, because of their understanding of fractions, know that 23/100 is 23 out of 100 equal parts; so they correctly interpret 0.23 as 23 out of 100 equal parts.

As students are given opportunities to model fractions and decimals, they observe that sometimes zeros are needed for the decimal form of a number to correctly represent a fractional value. For example, in figure 3.22, students see 5/100. To write this value as a decimal, they write a 0 in the tenths place to show that the value has no tenths, and they write 5 in the hundredths place. As students' understanding of the relationship between fractions and decimal places matures, they realize that 5/100 is written 0.05 and not 0.5 because in 0.5, the 5 is in the tenths place and means 5 tenths; the 5 must be in the hundredths place (0.05) to show 5 out of 100, or 5 hundredths.

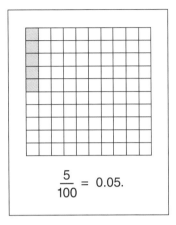

$$\frac{5}{100} = 0.05.$$

Fig. 3.22. Fraction model showing why 0 is written in the tenths place in the decimal form of 5/100

Also note that decimals less than 1 can be written with a 0 in the ones place, for example, 0.2 rather than .2. This practice is a convention that reinforces the relationship of the decimal point to the ones place and helps prevent the decimal point from being overlooked; however, .2 and 0.2 are both correct.

Just as fractions are used to represent values greater than 1, decimals are also used to describe values greater than 1. Students with a firm grasp of the equivalences between improper fractions and mixed numbers and a basic understanding of how fractions and decimals are related will find this concept relatively intuitive. Students use models like the one in figure 3.23 to understand how these relationships work together.

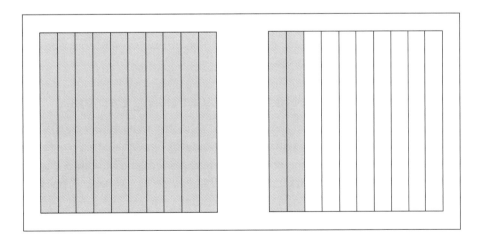

Fig. 3.23. Area models showing that $^{12}\!/_{10} = 1^{2}\!/_{10} = 1.2$

By thinking back to previous work with improper fractions and mixed numbers, students can interpret this model as $^{12}\!/_{10}$, or $1^{2}\!/_{10}$. As they develop the ability to relate fractions and decimals, students realize that $1^{2}\!/_{10} = 1 + {}^{2}\!/_{10}$, and that $^{2}\!/_{10}$ can also be written as 0.2. Thus, the goal is for them to assimilate all these concepts so as to understand that $^{12}\!/_{10} = 1^{2}\!/_{10} = 1.2$.

The number line is another familiar model that students can use to connect their understanding of fractions with decimal concepts. Using a number line to show decimals helps students begin to develop their sense of the relative magnitude of decimals, or how decimals are related to one another. For example, figure 3.24 illustrates that if students understand how to show tenths in fractional form on a number line, then they can also show the decimal forms of these fractions—0.1, 0.2, 0.3, 0.4, 0.5, and so on—in the appropriate places on the number line. As students develop their ability to show decimals on a number line, they can then use the number line to help them compare and order decimals and fractions.

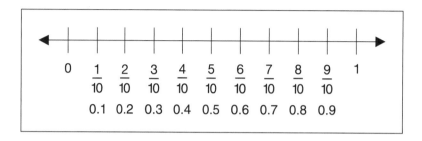

Fig. 3.24. Using a number line to relate fractions and decimals

In the same way that it is used in modeling whole numbers in earlier grades, the number-line model consists of a line that is divided by small vertical line segments that are labeled to show length from the zero point. The number-line model for fractions and decimals is a length model in which unit fractions (including decimal forms of tenths, hundredths, etc.) are marked as equal lengths between 0 and 1 (as well as between other consecutive whole numbers). However, the lengths can get "lost" visually, and students often focus on the marks between the whole numbers rather than the length from 0 to a given mark (or the length between two unit-fraction marks). Students who have difficulty creating or reading a number line labeled with fractions or decimals should be guided to identify the length that is being used (the distance from 0 to the point labeled with the fraction) by drawing a bar or thin oval from the beginning of the length (0) to the end of the length (the point labeled with the fraction). As with the number-line model for whole numbers, students need to focus on the lengths in the number-line model for fractions and decimals if they are to be able to use the number line to model operations with fractions and decimals in later grades.

Using fraction language to develop fluency in using decimals

Once students have begun to internalize the connection between fractions and decimals, they can begin to understand how to read and write decimals with understanding. As students learn to read decimals, they should connect decimal place value with the digits in a number, as they did in whole-number place value. For example, students might read the decimal number 6.17 as "six point one seven," but this way of reading the number does not indicate the value of each digit. Reading the number as "six and seventeen hundredths" or "six ones, 1 tenth, and 7 hundredths" is more meaningful. Although the latter way of reading the number is not the standard word form of the number, and is considered less efficient than the standard word form, it nevertheless provides information about the value of the digits in the number. Students can be encouraged to use the standard word form of a decimal, for example, "six and seventeen hundredths," by connecting the decimal parts of the number with what they have already learned about reading whole numbers. Also, conveniently, the last word said when the number is read in the standard word form indicates the place of the last digit. Thus, when students hear a number such as "twenty-three thousandths," they know to write "23" and that the 3 must be in the thousandths place. Similarly, if they see 0.023 and realize that the 3 is in the thousandths place, they know that they need to say "twenty-three" and then "thousandths" when they read the number.

Students should be aware that conventions for reading and writing decimals are not totally consistent. For example, some decimals that students will encounter in later grades cannot be read in standard word form, because the decimal representation is "nonterminating"; the number has no "last digit." An example of this phenomenon is the number 2/3, which is represented by a nonterminating repeating decimal that is written 0.6666…. The best way to read this number, then, is "zero point six six six and so forth."

Identifying equivalent decimals

Place-value notation and fractional understanding both can help students identify and write equivalent decimals. Students can use previously acquired knowledge about equivalent fractions to understand equivalent decimals. For example, in figure 3.25 the fraction 4/10 is represented by an area model and symbolically written as a fraction and a decimal. Students can use their knowledge of equivalent fractions to determine that 4/10 = 40/100. As their understanding of the relationship between fractions and decimals grows, they can reinterpret the models as showing that since 4/10 = 0.4 and 40/100 = 0.40, then 0.4 = 0.40.

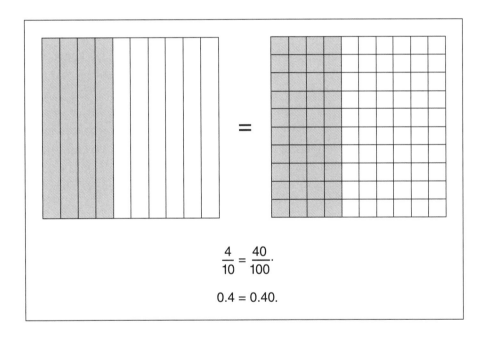

$$\frac{4}{10} = \frac{40}{100}.$$

$$0.4 = 0.40.$$

Fig. 3.25. Using fractional area models to illustrate equivalent decimals

Students can also use place value to understand equivalent decimals. As students are exposed to place-value charts as shown in figure 3.26, they begin to understand that 0.23 = 0.230 = 0.2300, and so on. This equivalence occurs because the zeros in the hundredths and thousandths places indicate that the number has no hundredths or thousandths, so including these zeros does not change the value of the number. Linking this concept with whole numbers will help students understand it, because it is not unlike writing zeros to the left of the first digit in a whole number, for example, 239 = 0239 = 00239. In 0239 and 00239, the zeros indicate that the number has no thousands and no ten thousandths, so including these zeros does not change the value of the number.

Ones		Tenths	Hundredths	Thousandths	Ten Thousandths	Hundred Thousandths
0	•	2	3			
0	•	2	3	0		
0	•	2	3	0	0	
0	•	2	3	0	0	0

Fig. 3.26. Using a place-value chart to illustrate equivalent decimals

The ability to use zeros to create equivalent decimals will be crucial as students learn how to use place value to compare and order decimals, as well as when they move on to adding and subtracting decimals with different numbers of decimal digits. For more information on determining fraction and decimal equivalence, refer to pages 41–48 of *Navigating through Number and Operations in Grades 3–5* (Duncan et al. 2007).

Comparing and ordering decimals

As students' understanding of decimals deepens, they begin to develop a more sophisticated sense of the relationships among tenths, hundredths, thousandths, and so on. For example, as figure 3.27 shows, tenths divide the whole into ten equal parts. So, for example, the marks on the tenths between 6 and 7 can be counted just as unit fractions can be counted: 6.1 (6 and 1/10), 6.2 (6 and 2/10), 6.3 (6 and 3/10), 6.4 (6 and 4/10), and so on through 6.9 (6 and 9/10). The 10th tenth coincides with a new whole, in this example, 6 and 10 tenths, or 7. In the same way, the hundredths divide the tenths into ten equal parts. So, for example, between 6.3 and 6.4 are 9 hundredths marks: 6.31, 6.32, 6.33, 6.34, and so on through 6.39. The 10th hundredth coincides with the next tenth, in this example, 6.4. The same is true for thousandths, for example, 6.321, 6.322, 6.323, 6.324, and so on through 6.329 occur between 6.32 and 6.33.

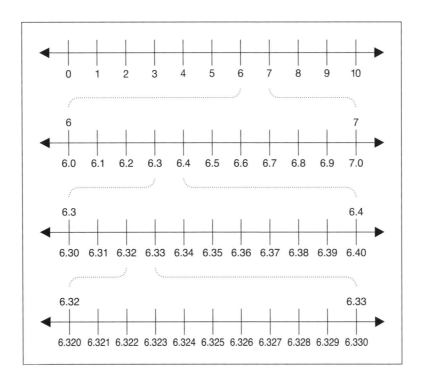

Fig. 3.27. "Zooming in" on portions of a number line to see tenths, hundredths, and thousandths

As figure 3.27 indicates, this process of "zooming in" between the tick marks on a number line can continue on to show ten thousandths, hundred thousandths, and so on. Students learn that the more parts into which a whole is divided, the smaller the parts; thus, tenths are larger than hundredths, hundredths are larger than thousandths, and so on. If students have a well-developed sense of this principle from fractions, the understanding of it in the context of decimals will be intuitive.

The discussion of comparing decimals includes both a connection with fractions as well as a connection with whole-number place value. Students can apply their understanding of equivalent fractions and comparing fractions with like denominators to understand how two nonequivalent decimal numbers are related to each other. For example, to compare 0.6 and 0.7, students can think of 0.6 as 6/10 and 0.7 as 7/10. From their work with fractions, they know fewer tenths are in 6/10 than in 7/10, so 6/10 < 7/10 and therefore, 0.6 < 0.7.

Students can also apply their understanding of equivalent fractions to compare decimals. For example, when asked to compare 0.8 and 0.17, students who do not understand decimals as fractions often make the error that 0.8 < 0.17 because 8 < 17. However, students who understand decimals as fractions think of 8/10 and 17/100. Then they can use their knowledge of equivalent fractions to determine that 8/10 = 80/100. Once they have established this equivalence, they can clearly see that 80/100 > 17/100, so 0.8 > 0.17. Students can also compare decimals that are mixed numbers. For example, to compare 3.26 and 2.9, students need only look at the whole-number part of the decimals, just as they would if they were to compare $3\frac{26}{100}$ and $2\frac{9}{10}$. Because 3 > 2, 3.26 > 2.9. As students move to decimals with the same whole-number part, they learn that they need to compare only the decimal part of the number. So, for example, to compare 5.03 and 5.1, they need to compare 0.03 and 0.1. As described previously, they can think of the fractions 3/100 and 1/10. They know that 1/10 = 10/100, so they can determine that 3/100 < 10/100, so 0.03 < 0.1 and therefore, 5.03 < 5.1. Thus, a solid foundation of writing equivalent fractions, comparing fractions with the same denominator, and knowing how fractions and decimals are related work together to help students learn how to compare decimals.

To facilitate the development of fluency in decimal concepts, students need to understand how to use decimal place value as well as their knowledge of decimal-fractional equivalence to compare decimals. After using number lines and fractions with common denominators as described previously to compare decimal numbers, students can apply their knowledge of comparing whole numbers to comparing decimals. For example, when students used place value to compare whole numbers in grade 3, they first needed to consider the greatest place in each number. They apply this same reasoning when comparing decimals. In the examples in figure 3.28, students can use the greatest place in each number to compare the numbers.

Comparison	Reasoning
A. 1.01 > 0.99.	Wholes are greater than tenths, so 1.01 is greater than 0.99.
B. 0.3 > 0.098.	Tenths are greater than hundredths, so 0.3 is greater than 0.098.
C. 86.9 < 102.1.	Tens are less than hundreds, so 86.9 is less than 102.1.

Fig. 3.28. Examples of comparing decimals by considering the greatest place value in each number

As students' study of comparing continues, they will encounter decimals in which the largest place in each number is the same. Students can also use their understanding of whole-number place value to compare such numbers. For example, if students need to compare 5.96 and 5.93, they realize that the largest place in each number is the ones place. So then they begin comparing the values of the digits in each place from left to right starting with the largest place, the ones place: 5 ones = 5 ones, so they move to the next-largest place, the tenths place. They know that 9 tenths = 9 tenths, so they move to the next-largest place, the hundredths place. Because 6 hundredths is greater than 3 hundredths, they know that 5.96 > 5.93. Thus, a solid foundation in comparing whole numbers coupled with a basic understanding of decimal place values will enable students to use place value to compare decimal numbers.

Strengthening Fluency through Connections

As described throughout this Focal Point, students use the connection between fractions and decimals to develop and understand decimal concepts. This connection solidifies students' understanding of decimals and their relationship to fractions and whole numbers. Figure 3.29 shows some of the common fraction-decimal equivalences that students will encounter in grade 4; however, other useful equivalences will be discovered in later grades, including nonterminating decimals. Fluency in the automatic recall of these equivalences will facilitate students' work with more sophisticated mathematical topics, such as ratio and percent.

$$\frac{1}{2} = 0.5 \qquad \frac{1}{4} = 0.25 \qquad \frac{3}{4} = 0.75$$

$$\frac{1}{10} = 0.1 \quad \frac{2}{10} = 0.2 \quad \frac{3}{10} = 0.3 \quad \frac{4}{10} = 0.4 \quad \frac{5}{10} = 0.5 \quad \frac{6}{10} = 0.6 \quad \frac{7}{10} = 0.7 \quad \frac{8}{10} = 0.8 \quad \frac{9}{10} = 0.9$$

$$\frac{1}{5} = 0.2 \qquad \frac{2}{5} = 0.4 \qquad \frac{3}{5} = 0.6 \qquad \frac{4}{5} = 0.8$$

Fig. 3.29. Common equivalent fractions and decimals

Students can also connect fractions and decimals with monetary situations. Showing how to express a fraction of a dollar in terms of cents will allow students who have a solid understanding of money to further conceptualize fractions and decimals. For example, 100 pennies are in 1 dollar, so 1 penny is 1/100 of a dollar, or equal to 1¢, or $0.01. Students can use this knowledge to write fractions as decimals. For example, 57 pennies is equal to 57/100 of a dollar, or $0.57, so 57/100 = 0.57. Students can extend this reasoning to use other coins to identify equivalent fractions and decimals. For example, 10 dimes are in 1 dollar, so each dime is 1/10 of a dollar. If students know that the value of a dime is 10¢, or $0.10, then they have illustrated the equivalence 10/100 = 1/10 = 0.1, 20/100 = 2/10 = 0.2, 30/100 = 3/10 = 0.3, and so on. Students can illustrate other equivalences using the quarter and the nickel, (e.g., 25/100 = 0.25 and 5/100 = 0.05). Students can also extend this basic understanding to explore more sophisticated relationships. For example, students know that a quarter is equal to 25¢, or 25/100. Students who understand that, because 4 quarters are in 1 dollar, a quarter is 1/4 of a dollar can expand their knowledge of equivalences to include 1/4 = 25/100 = 0.25. Students can use this same understanding and reasoning to find that 1/2 = 0.5, 1/5 = 0.20, 3/4 = 0.75, and so on.

Another powerful connection that can be made is between decimals and metric measurement. The metric system of measurement and the base-ten number system are both based on powers of 10. Thus, students can connect the decimal place values with the units of metric measurement. As shown in figure 3.30, 1 meter is divided into 10 parts, called *decimeters*. Each decimeter is 1/10 of a meter. One decimeter is divided into 10 parts, called *centimeters*. Each centimeter is 1/100 of a meter. A centimeter is divided into 10 parts, called *millimeters*. Each millimeter is 1/1000 of a meter. As students use the metric system, they notice parallels between these metric measurements and the decimal place values. They see that meters are like ones, decimeters are like tenths, centimeters are like hundredths, and millimeters are like thousandths. Students can then use this connection to interpret lengths written as decimals. For example 1.2 meters is 1 meter and 2 decimeters; 1.23 meters is 1 meter, 2 decimeters, and 3 centimeters; and 1.234 meters is 1 meter, 2 decimeters, 3 centimeters, and 4 millimeters.

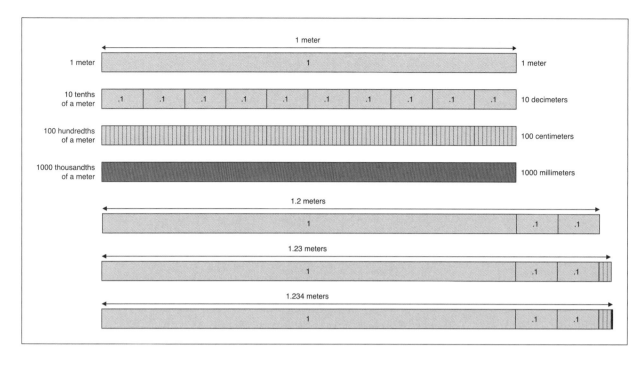

Fig. 3.30. Model illustrating the connection between metric units of measure and decimal numbers

Connections in Later Grades

In grade 5, students will expand the relationship between fractions and decimals as they connect division and fractions. In this grade they learn that every fraction in the form a/b, where b is not equal to 0, can be interpreted as $a \div b$. Students can then use division to translate any fraction with a whole-number numerator and a whole-number denominator not equal to zero into an equivalent decimal. As students progress into more sophisticated mathematics, they will learn that fractions of the form a/b where a and b are integers and b is not equal to 0 are called *rational numbers*. Students will also learn that although every rational number can be written as a decimal, not every decimal is a rational number. For example, students will learn that nonrepeating, nonterminating decimals (also called *irrational numbers*) cannot be written in fraction form as a/b where a and b are integers and b is not equal to 0.

In grade 5, students will use and apply their understanding of fractions developed in grades 3 and 4 as they learn how to add and subtract fractions with like and unlike denominators. In addition, students continue to develop the foundational understanding of decimals presented in grade 4 as they explore decimal place value through the millionths place in grade 5. Students will apply this understanding as they learn to add and subtract decimals.

Measuring Depth of Understanding

In this Focal Point, students developed an understanding of the connection between fractions and decimals. Explain how students could use this model to represent both a fraction and a decimal.

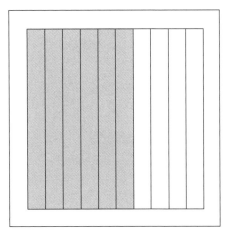

Focusing on Area of Two-Dimensional Shapes

In grade 4, students continue to develop and deepen their understanding of two-dimensional shapes. The focus in grade 4 is on estimating, describing, analyzing, and calculating the area of two-dimensional shapes. Students will learn to use multiplication to find the area of a rectangle. Students will also use the concepts of composing and decomposing two-dimensional shapes to help them as they learn about area and how to determine the total area of complex shapes. In addition, students will apply their understanding of congruence and symmetry as they explore transformations and tessellations and will apply these understandings to area.

Instructional Progression for the Area of Two-Dimensional Shapes

The focus on the concept of area and the properties of two-dimensional shapes in grade 4 is supported by a progression of related mathematical ideas before and after grade 4, as shown in table 4.1. To give perspective to the grade 4 work, we first discuss some of the important ideas that students focus on in grade 3 that prepare them for this learning in grade 4. At the end of the detailed discussion of this grade 4 Focal Point, we present examples of how students will use the concept of area and the related skills in later grades. For more detailed discussions of the "before" and "after" parts of the instructional progression, please see the appropriate grade-level books, that is, *Focus in Grade 3* (NCTM 2009) and *Focus in Grade 5* (NCTM 2009).

Table 4.1 represents an instructional progression for the understanding of area and the properties of two- (and three-) dimensional shapes in grades 3 through 5.

Early Foundations

Early foundations for understanding two-dimensional shapes

In their study of geometric concepts in grade 3, students begin to formalize the language used to analyze and classify shapes. For example, students use *polygon* to describe simple, closed shapes with straight sides, *angle* to describe the corners, and *vertex* to describe the "points at the corners" of those shapes and learn how to identify an angle as right, acute, or obtuse. Students use their comprehension of these angle concepts to identify, classify, and describe geometric shapes when, for example, they articulate that rectangles (including squares) are distinguishable from other quadrilaterals because they have four right angles.

In grade 3, students also learn how to describe quadrilaterals by considering the angles and side lengths and relationships among the sides. The Venn diagram in figure 4.1, although not presented to students at this level, illustrates the embedded relationships among quadrilateral classifications. As students learn the properties of each type of quadrilateral, they begin to internalize these relationships.

Table 4.1
Grade 4: Focusing on Area of Two-Dimensional Shapes
Instructional Progression for Developing Understanding in Grades 3–5

Grade 3	Grade 4	Grade 5
Students build, draw, and analyze two-dimensional shapes to explore their attributes and properties. Students describe, analyze, compare, and classify two-dimensional shapes by their sides and angles. Students decompose, combine, and transform polygons to make other polygons to build foundations for area and fraction models. Students solve problems involving congruence and symmetry. Students build, draw, and analyze two-dimensional shapes to understand their attributes and properties.	Students recognize area as an attribute of two-dimensional regions. Students learn that they can quantify area by finding the total number of same-sized units of area that cover a shape without gaps or overlaps. Students understand that a square that is 1 unit on a side is the standard unit for measuring area. Students select appropriate units, strategies (e.g, decomposing shapes), and tools to solve problems involving estimating or measuring area. Students make the connection between area and the area model that they have used to represent multiplication to justify the formula for the area of a rectangle.	Students relate two-dimensional shapes to three-dimensional shapes. Students analyze properties of polyhedral solids, describing them by the number of edges, faces, or vertices as well as the types of faces. Students recognize volume as an attribute of three-dimensional space. Students understand that they can quantify volume by finding the total number of same-sized units of volume that they need to fill the space without gaps or overlaps. Students understand that a cube that is 1 unit on an edge is the standard unit for measuring volume. Students decompose three-dimensional shapes to build foundations for computing volume. Students find surface areas and volumes of prisms. Students use the relationships of different polygons to rectangles to find and justify the formulas for the areas of the different polygons. Students identify and measure the attributes of shapes needed to use area formulas to solve problems.

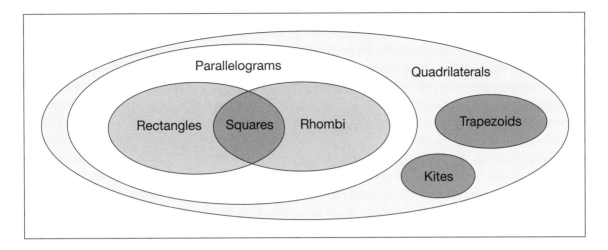

Fig. 4.1. Venn diagram illustrating the embedded relationship among quadrilaterals

In grade 3, students also formalize the intuitive concept of "same size, same shape" when they learn that when two shapes are the same size and shape, they are *congruent*. The concept of congruence is interwoven throughout many of the geometric concepts that students encounter, both in grade 3 and in later grades. For example, to classify polygons, students consider whether the sides of the shape are congruent and whether the angles are congruent. To identify the properties of a shape, students also consider congruence. For example, a quadrilateral is a rhombus if all its sides are congruent, and a triangle is isosceles if at least two of its sides are congruent. In grade 4, students apply their understanding of congruence in more sophisticated situations, for example, when students learn about various types of geometric transformations, such as a rotation (or turn), in which the resulting shape is congruent to the original shape. Congruence also continues to be used by students as they expand their understanding of area in grade 4, when, for example, they learn that they can quantify the area of a shape by finding the number of congruent square units that are needed to cover the shape.

In grade 3, students apply their understanding of congruence as they learn about symmetry. Students learn that if a shape has line symmetry, a line, called a *line of symmetry,* can be drawn that divides the shape into two congruent parts, as shown in figure 4.2. The shapes at the left in the figure have at least one line of symmetry, so they have line symmetry.

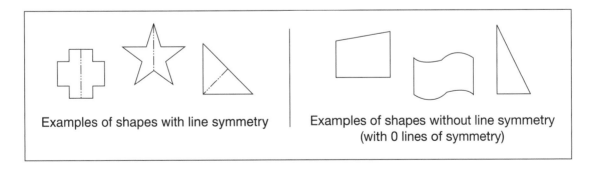

Examples of shapes with line symmetry | Examples of shapes without line symmetry (with 0 lines of symmetry)

Fig. 4.2. Examples of shapes with and without line symmetry

Students can use inspection, mirrors, and paper folding to explore whether a shape has a line of symmetry. Just as they did in working with congruence, students need to note that none of the acts of inspection, paper folding, or using mirrors actually proves that a figure has line symmetry, because our senses are not exact. However, these techniques can help students understand the meaning of line symmetry. As students fold shapes, they internalize that if a folded shape has a line of symmetry, the edges of two parts match exactly when the shape is folded on the line of symmetry. Through many concrete and pictorial experiences, students realize that shapes can have from zero to an infinite number of lines of symmetry (as in the instance of a circle). Students apply the concept of symmetry as they use reflections and rotations to determine and produce line and rotational symmetry in grade 4.

Early foundations for understanding area

In grade 3, students apply the composition and decomposition of geometric shapes to multiplication. This exploration provides students with the foundation they will need to understand the area concepts presented in grade 4. For example, in figure 4.3, students interpret the area model as a 2-by-4 array consisting of 8 squares in all. As students link their understanding of combining and decomposing shapes with models for multiplication, they begin to see that the model is, in fact, a rectangle decomposed into rows of adjacent squares. They can multiply the number of rows by the number of columns to find the total number of squares in all. Initially students interpret this decomposed shape as an area model illustrating that 2 groups of 4, or 2 × 4, equals 8. As they mature in their understanding of area concepts, they will associate the connected array with a 2-unit-by-4-unit rectangle having an area of 8 square units. The work that they have done in multiplication will allow them to realize that they can multiply the numbers of units in the dimensions to find the area.

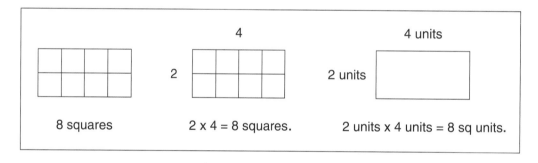

Fig. 4.3. Example that illustrates the progression from the multiplication area model to the calculation of area

Students can also apply their understanding of arrays of squares as decomposed rectangles to understand multiplication properties. For example, as illustrated in figure 4.4, students can see that the rectangle can be decomposed into squares that are arranged to show an array with 4 rows and 3 squares in each row and then these squares can be arranged in another way to show an array with the same size and shape and that has 3 rows and 4 squares in each row. Thus, if students know that they can multiply the length times the width to find the number of squares in an array, they can use the decomposition in this model to show the commutative property, or that 4 × 3 = 3 × 4. Students apply this understanding as they learn that a rectangle that is 3 units by 4 units has the same area, and when considered in the abstract, is the same rectangle as a rectangle that is 4 units by 3 units.

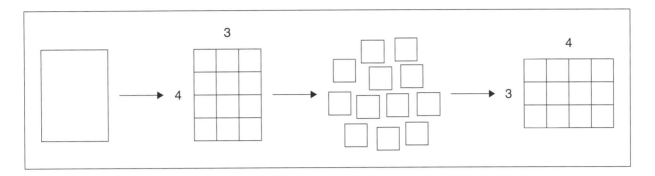

Fig. 4.4. Example illustrating how decomposition and combining can be
applied to the commutative property of multiplication

Students can also use decomposition to understand the distributive property of multiplication over addition. As illustrated in figure 4.5, students can see that because the rectangle has been decomposed into an array with 4 rows and 3 squares in each row, it can be decomposed further to show 2 rectangles each with 2 rows and 3 squares in each row. Thus, the model shows that $4 \times 3 = (2 + 2) \times 3 = (2 \times 3) + (2 \times 3)$.

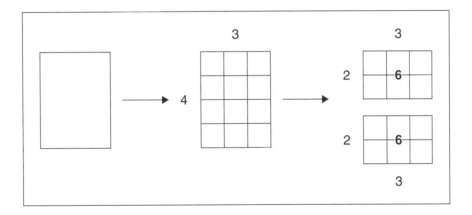

Fig. 4.5. Example illustrating how decomposition can be applied to the
distributive property of multiplication over addition

Students apply this ability to visualize the decomposed rectangle as two smaller rectangles to help them learn how to decompose complex shapes into simple shapes to find the area. For example, students can apply the illustration shown in figure 4.5 to find the area of the larger 4 by 3 rectangle by finding the areas of the smaller 2 by 3 rectangles and adding those areas. For further details on the grade 3 focal point Focusing on Two-Dimensional Shapes, refer to *Focus in Grade 3* (NCTM 2009).

Building Understanding of Area

The meaning of area as a measurable attribute

In grade 4, students begin to realize the need for the concept of area as a measurable attribute. This need is prompted by the desire to compare the sizes of two-dimensional shapes and to describe the size of such shapes succinctly to others. When, for example, students are presented with the situation as shown in figure 4.6, in which one of two rectangular plots of land is wider but shorter than the other, and are asked to decide which plot is "larger," students realize that which plot of land is larger is not immediately obvious. Experiences such as these lead students to realize that the measurements about which they have previously learned, that is, length, width, weight or mass, and capacity, are insufficient ways to compare and describe the "size" of these shapes. They have a need to quantify the size of the shapes using another type of measurement, and thus the conceptual framework needed to begin their discussion about area measurement is formed.

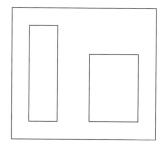

Fig. 4.6. Examples of rectangular plots of land used to discuss the need for measuring area

As students begin their study of area, they learn that the area of a two-dimensional shape is a measure of the amount of material needed to cover the shape. Just as students learned about linear measurement by first using nonstandard units, such as paper clips, to measure length, students should be given opportunities to use nonstandard units as they first begin to explore the measurement of area. For example, students should place smaller objects of different sizes and shapes on top of larger objects to determine about how many of the smaller objects are needed to cover the larger object with no overlap and the fewest gaps possible. Thus, students may first approximate the area of objects in, for example, pennies, pattern blocks, or square tiles, as shown in figure 4.7. Students could then describe the rectangle as having an area of about 20 pennies, 9 hexagons, or 12 square tiles.

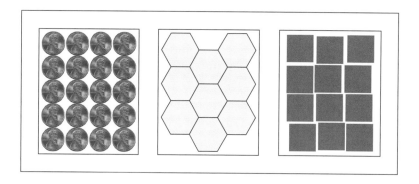

Fig. 4.7. Using nonstandard units to approximate the area of an object

In addition to students using nonstandard units to explore area, students' initial experiences with area should also involve using informal methods to compare the areas of two-dimensional shapes. For example, in figure 4.8 students see three different rectangles, A, B, and C. To determine which rectangle is the largest, students learn that they can compare the area of the shapes by folding the shapes into equal-sized pieces and comparing the number of those pieces in each shape. For example, students might fold rectangle C into four congruent horizontal pieces and realize that rectangle A is a different shape but is also composed of four of the same-sized pieces, so the area of C is the same as the area of A. Students could also fold rectangle C into three congruent vertical pieces or fold it both horizontally and vertically to reach the same conclusion. When students make these folds on C, they are able to use the resulting rectangles or squares as common, but still nonstandard, units to show that rectangles A and C cover the same amount of space. Students can repeat the process to compare rectangles A and B and rectangles B and C.

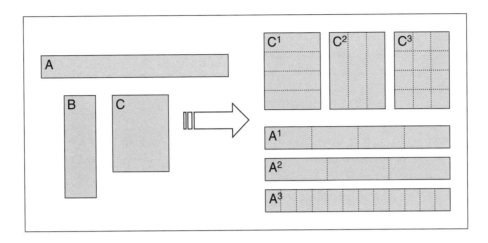

Fig. 4.8. Example of using "same-sized" pieces to compare area

Although this initial area work involves only whole numbers of units, students will eventually work with shapes that involve fractions of square units. Students may want to cut such shapes apart and rearrange the parts to form whole-unit squares. Introductory activities such as these help students to continue to develop an understanding of area and motivate them to realize the need for standard units of area. In figure 4.8, the shapes have the same area and the equal-sized pieces fit perfectly within each shape. However, as students continue to have opportunities to compare areas, they begin to realize the need for a standard unit of measure that can be used in every situation. Another benefit of these types of explorations is that students begin to understand that even though rectangles have different shapes, they can have the same area.

As students are given many opportunities to experiment with measuring area using different types of shapes for units of area, they will learn by observation that using certain types of units of area results in more efficient and exact measurements than using others. In figure 4.7, students observe that the circular and hexagonal shapes are not very exact units to use to measure the area of a rectangular shape because, in each example, the units do not entirely cover the shape. Through such experiences, students learn that squares make especially exact and efficient units of area because they fit together snugly to completely cover a rectangular shape and can be arranged in rows and columns as a type of rectangular array. As students' knowledge of area progresses, they learn that standard units of area are square. Students learn that, for example, square inches and square centimeters can be used to measure areas of small shapes, such as those that students can draw on a piece of notebook paper or see in a textbook. Figure 4.9 shows a square centimeter and a square inch.

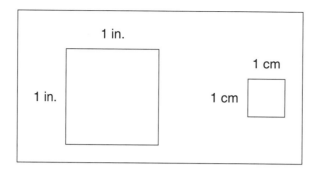

Fig. 4.9. One square inch and 1 square centimeter

To measure larger areas, such as the area of the classroom, students learn that a square meter, a square yard, or a square foot can be used. To measure even greater areas, for example, the size of a state or town, students learn that a square kilometer or a square mile might be used. Regardless of the unit chosen, students learn that the area of a shape, in square units, is the number of 1-unit-by-1-unit squares (*unit squares*) needed to cover the shape without gaps or overlaps. Inside the shape shown in figure 4.10 are 25 square units, so students learn that the area of the shape is 25 square units. If the units were square inches, the area would be 25 square inches; if the units were square meters, the area would be 25 square meters, and so on.

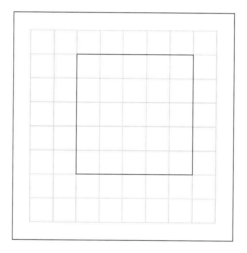

Fig. 4.10. Illustration of a shape with an area of 25 square units

Finding the area of rectangles

Once students understand the meaning of area as a measurable attribute, they can then begin to explore the areas of specific shapes, such as rectangles. In grade 4, students use the formula $A = l \times w$ to find the area of rectangles. They need to use investigative techniques so that they can make connections between the characteristics of the rectangle and the symbols to understand this formula. For example, students can make rectangles with square tiles and count the tiles to determine the area in square tiles. Then they can make an organized presentation of the length, width, and area of each rectangle and analyze the relationships among the numbers. Figure 4.11 shows typical results from this activity. Through opportunities such as the one illustrated in figure 4.11, students are able to begin to understand that for every rectangle, the product of the length and the width is equal to the area.

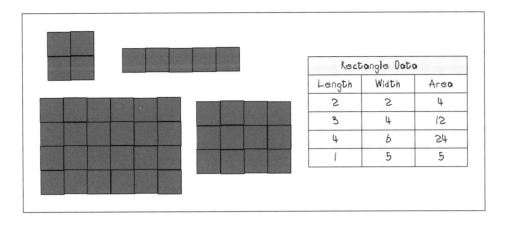

Fig. 4.11. Activity to illustrate the connections among length, width, and area of a rectangle

To further develop their conceptual framework for the formula for the area of a rectangle, students connect the rectangle with the understanding of decomposition that they developed in grade 3. In grade 3, students decomposed a rectangle into arrays of adjacent squares. They learned that they could find the number of squares inside the array by counting them. This method is similar to counting the square units inside a figure to determine its area. In grade 3, however, students then connected the array model with multiplication. They learned how to see the array shown in figure 4.12 as 5 rows (or groups) with 3 in each group. Thus, students learned that they could use the mathematical process of multiplication, rather than count one by one, as a more efficient way to find the total number of squares in the array. Students in grade 4 learn to interpret such arrays of adjacent squares as the squares that could be composed to form a rectangle. Thus, students can use their previously acquired understanding to realize that they can use multiplication as a mathematical process for quickly counting the unit squares needed to cover the rectangle; in other words, they can multiply the length times the width to find the area of the rectangle.

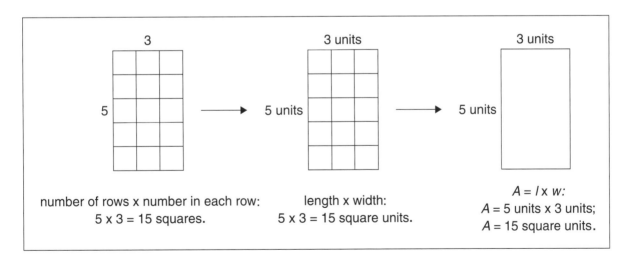

Fig. 4.12. Conceptual progression from decomposing a rectangle to an array, to using multiplication to find the number of squares in the array, to using the area formula to find the area of a rectangle

As students synthesize their learning from grade 3, they realize that the number of rows in the array is like the length (or width) of the rectangle. The number of squares in each row is like the width (or length). If, to find the number of squares in an array, students multiply the number of rows by the number in each row, then to find the number of square units in the rectangle, students multiply the number of units in the length by the number of units in the width. This connection leads to an understanding of the formula for finding the area of a rectangle ($A = l \times w$). Teachers should emphasize to students that because the commutative property of multiplication states that numbers can be multiplied in any order to get the same product, in a rectangle, which dimension is designated as the length and which is designated as the width does not matter.

Through a variety of experiences, including experiences with lengths and widths that are larger numbers, in which students find areas of different rectangles, students begin to realize that using the length-times-width formula to find the areas of rectangles is a more efficient strategy than counting squares one by one, and it can be a powerful tool for efficiently and accurately finding areas in problem-solving situations.

After students have had the opportunity to explore area, they will gain a deeper appreciation for the reason that the standard units used to measure area are square. They learn that, because squares have four right angles and four congruent sides, squares fit together snuggly to form uniform rows and columns that, in turn, allow multiplication to be used as a quick method of counting the squares. Although all students' initial experiences with area should be concrete and pictorial, students in grade 4 are expected to move to using the abstract formula to find the area of rectangles. Because students will make this progression at varying rates, concrete experiences that include square tiles and grid paper should continue until students have made the meaningful transition from the concrete to the abstract.

Other units of area

As students move from measuring the area of shapes that can be created, drawn, or pictured on paper or on a desktop to larger shapes in the world around them, they begin to see the need for larger units of area. Students move to using square feet, square meters, square miles, square kilometers, and so on. Students need to understand the relationship between a smaller unit of area and a larger unit. For example, by presenting the units as shown in figure 4.13, students visualize that because 12 inches are in a foot, a square foot is composed of a 12-by-12 array of square inches; thus, a square foot is 12×12, or 144, square inches. Students should be presented with similar illustrations to show relationships between other square units, for example, that because 100 centimeters are in a meter, a square meter is composed of a 100-by-100 array of square centimeters, and so a square meter is composed of 100×100, or 10,000, square centimeters.

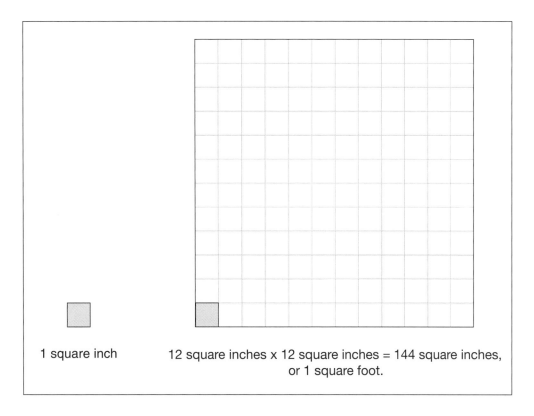

1 square inch   12 square inches x 12 square inches = 144 square inches,
                                            or 1 square foot.

Fig. 4.13. Illustration comparing 1 square inch and 1 square foot

Through concrete and pictorial experiences with larger shapes, students realize that any area can be measured in large or small units of area; however, one type of unit of area may be more appropriate than another. For example, students will observe that they may not wish to measure the area of their state using square centimeters, because they would need to use so many of them. Because square kilometers are much larger, a more reasonable number of square kilometers than square centimeters are needed to measure such a large area. The discussion about which unit to choose to measure different amounts of area is very important for students to engage in as they develop measurement sense. Also, they will apply these understandings later as they explore precision in measurement.

As was true when students studied measurement in previous grades, when considering area in real-world situations in grade 4, students must begin to develop the ability to estimate. Students begin this process as they consider which unit of area measure is the most appropriate to use to measure certain areas. However, hands-on experiences that include predicting measurements and then finding actual measurements facilitate students' development of a sense of the size of each unit of area.

Strengthening understanding of area through problem solving

Using area and the understanding of the properties of other two-dimensional shapes to solve problems can help students better understand the concept of area and its applications. The strategies students use to solve the problems will vary, depending on their comprehension of area, as well as the extent to which they understand the properties of two-dimensional shapes.

One example of a problem-solving situation in which students apply their understanding of area and the properties of two-dimensional shapes is in finding the area of complex shapes. For example, a group of students in grade 4 was asked to find the area of the complex shape shown in figure 4.14.

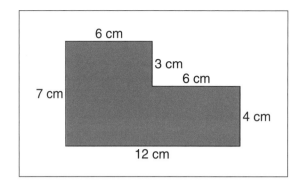

Fig. 4.14. Complex shape of which students were asked to find the area

The following discussion between the teacher and the students shows that students with varying degrees of understanding solved the problem in different ways and that the discussion of the various strategies contributed to each student's understanding.

Teacher: Mia, how did you find the area?

Mia: I traced the shape on the grid paper, and luckily, the corners fit right on the corners of the grid! Then I counted the number of squares that were in the shape. There were 66 squares in the shape, so I knew that the shape was 66 square centimeters.

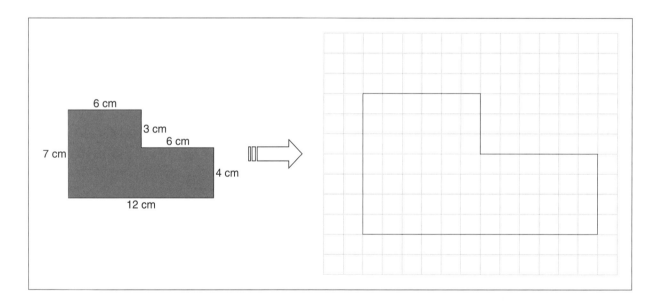

Fig. 4.14. One student's solution to the area problem using grid squares

Teacher: And that is exactly what area means—how many square units of area does it take to completely cover a shape? Did anyone do it in a way where they didn't have to count the squares separately?

Samara: I did. I used square tiles to make the shape, but then instead of counting them, I saw that I could make two rectangles. I used multiplication to find the areas of these two rectangles, and then I added these areas together to get 66 square centimeters.

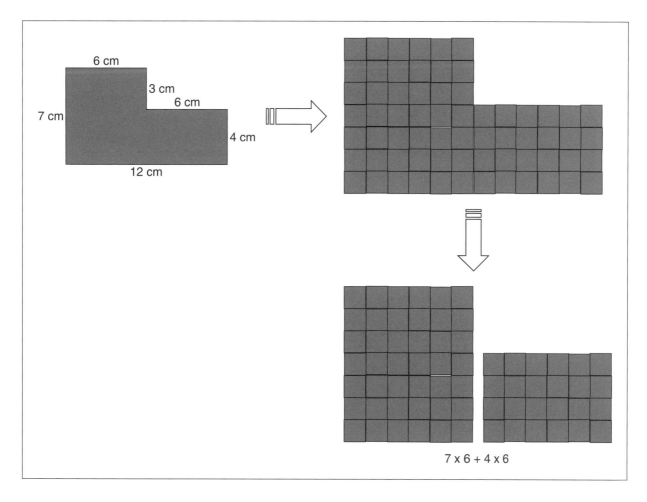

Fig. 4.15. Another student's solution to the area problem using grid-square rectangles

Teacher: Samara, how did you know that you could divide the large shape into smaller shapes?

Samara: Well, I know that if you just break apart a shape into smaller shapes, you don't change the area. So you can find the areas of the smaller pieces and add them together to find the area of the large piece.

Teacher: How did you know what numbers to multiply to find the areas of the smaller rectangles?

Samara: I used the edges of the tiles to find the length and width of each rectangle.

Tomas: Samara, I divided the shape into rectangles to find the area, too, but I didn't use grid paper or square tiles. I just used a line, like we did in third grade. Remember, you can divide shapes up in lots of different ways. After I drew the line, I used the area formula to multiply to find the area of each rectangle and got 18 square centimeters and 48 square centimeters. I added these together and got 66 square centimeters for the whole thing, just like you did, Samara. [See fig. 4.16.]

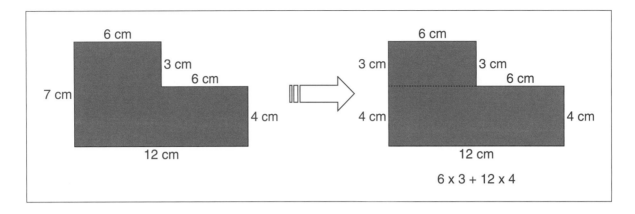

Fig. 4.16. Another student's solution to the area problem using rectangle measurements

Teacher: Is anyone surprised that Mia and Samara and Tomas all got the same answer?

Several students simultaneously: No, it's just different ways to get the same thing. They're all areas of the same shape. It doesn't matter how you take it apart, as long as you don't lose any or add any.

Teacher: Tomas, why didn't you copy your shape onto grid paper or use square tiles to make the shape?

Tomas: Because I can use the numbers that are on the diagram to figure out how many grid squares there would be on each side, so I just multiplied the right numbers to find the areas.

Joanne: I solved it a different way. I saw that I could put two of these shapes together to make a big rectangle. Then I found the area of the big rectangle and divided it by 2. [See fig. 4.17.]

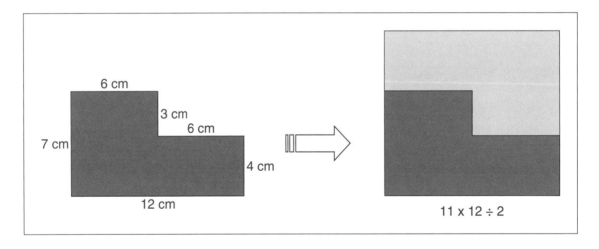

Fig. 4.17. Another student's solution to the area problem using a large rectangle

Teacher: And why did you divide the area of the big rectangle by 2?

Joanne: Because there were two of the shapes in the big rectangle, and I just wanted the area of one of them.

Teacher: Matthew, how did you find the area?

Matthew: I used a different way than everyone else. The shape is like a rectangle with a little piece missing. So I found the area of the "filled-in" rectangle and the area of the "hole" part and then subtracted the hole from the filled-in rectangle. [See fig. 4.18.]

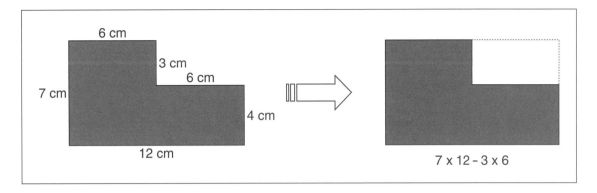

Fig. 4.18. Student's solution using a subtract-the-"hole" strategy

Teacher: Why did you subtract the area of the smaller piece from the bigger piece?

Matthew: Because you need to take the smaller part away from the bigger part, like cutting it out with a pair of scissors, to leave the part you want.

As is clear from this discussion, less confident students may rely more at first on concrete materials, such as grid paper and square tiles, to solve area problems. Students who have developed a deeper understanding of area and the properties of two-dimensional shapes will use more abstract methods to find solutions. An important aspect to note is that during the discussion, the teacher prompted students to explain their thinking and guided them through the progression of the different strategies that each student used. Students benefit from connecting the early representations using models with the more sophisticated strategies.

Understanding relationships among methods used and the ways to visualize shapes to solve problems involving area leads to a deeper understanding of the area of complex figures. In all representations, if students implement their strategies effectively, they will find the correct solution. However, one of the goals of this Focal Point is for students to move from a concrete understanding of the area of a rectangle to an abstract one in which students effectively use a formula. Also, as students explore different methods of finding the area of complex shapes, and construct the corresponding numerical expressions for the methods of their choice, they begin to see the purpose for using variables and the relationships between expressions that may look different but are equivalent mathematically, each of which are essential foundations for algebra.

Perimeter and area

Another way in which students can strengthen their understanding of area and of the properties of two-dimensional figures is by comparing and contrasting different types of measurements. In grade 3, students learned about linear measurement, including perimeter. In grade 4, students assimilate their previous understanding of these two concepts with their emerging understanding of area to solve problems that involve comparing and analyzing the relationships of the areas and perimeters of different figures. For example, students can use concrete and pictorial models to answer the question "Can figures with the same perimeters have different areas?" As students are given opportunities to explore this question, they begin to realize that the answer to this question is yes. After several experiences, students can be led to synthesize their understandings of area, perimeter, and the properties of two-dimensional shapes by observing that if the lengths of two adjacent sides of a rectangle add to half the perimeter of the rectangle, any rectangle in which the sum of the width and the length is 6 will have a perimeter of 12 units. Thus, they realize that a 5-unit-by-1-unit rectangle, a 4-unit-by-2-unit rectangle, a 3-unit-by-3-unit rectangle, and a 1½-unit-by-4½-unit rectangle all have the same perimeter but different areas. In figure 4.19, rectangle A has an area of 5 square units, rectangle B's area is 8 square units, rectangle C's area is 9 square units, and rectangle D's area is $6\frac{3}{4}$ square units. Note that although students at grade 4 are not yet multiplying decimals or fractions, they can use the grid paper to determine the area of the rectangle with fractional dimensions.

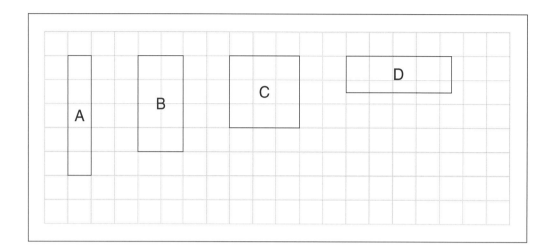

Fig. 4.19. Examples illustrating that shapes can have the same perimeter but different areas

Students also can use concrete and pictorial models, such as grid paper and square tiles, to answer the question "Can figures with the same areas have different perimeters?" They soon learn that the answer to this question is yes, as well. For example, as students arrange 24 square tiles in as many rectangular arrays as they can, they observe that the area of each rectangle is 24 square units but each rectangle has a different perimeter. Some of the rectangles that can be created with 24 tiles are shown in figure 4.20. These examples clearly show that the areas of the rectangles are the same but the perimeters are different.

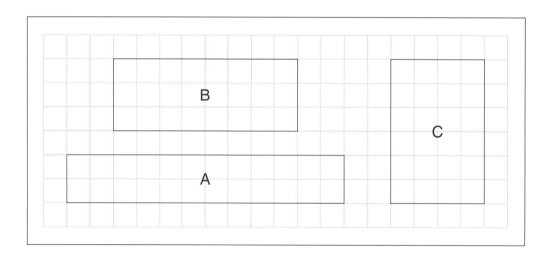

Fig. 4.20. Examples illustrating that shapes can have the same areas but different perimeters

As students explore these types of questions, they not only deepen their understanding of the concepts of area and perimeter but also gain experience in reasoning through the creation of examples and counterexamples.

Strengthening Fluency through Connections

Students must be exposed to and understand connections among mathematics concepts. This foundation leads to a deeper understanding of mathematics and how concepts build on one another and are related both within a grade level and across grade levels. Connections with other mathematical concepts at this grade level are evident throughout this Focal Point. In the grade 4 Connections to the Focal Points, several geometric concepts are introduced as preparation for future Focal Points. The following connections, all related to spatial geometry, continue to develop students' understanding of the properties of two-dimensional figures.

Transformations, symmetry, and congruence

In grade 4, students learn formal language for certain transformations: flips are *reflections,* slides are *translations,* and turns are *rotations,* as illustrated in figure 4.21. As students are given opportunities to transform, or move, a variety of concrete and pictorial shapes, they learn that these three types of transformations never change the size or the shape of an object; in other words, the original object and the result of the transformation of the object are congruent.

Description	Example
Translation Result of sliding a shape to a new location	
Reflection Result of flipping a shape over a line, which is called the *line of reflection*	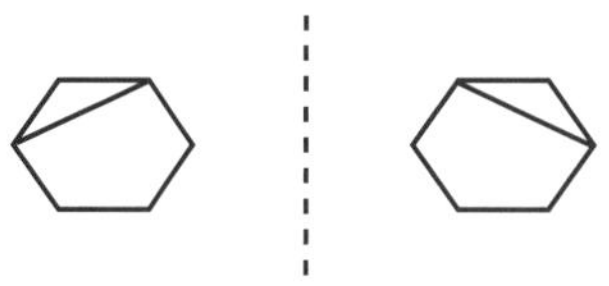
Rotation Result of turning a shape about a point	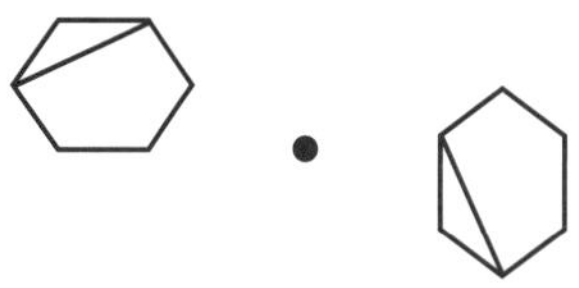

Fig. 4.21. Descriptions and examples of figures and their images resulting from transformations

Students then connect their understanding of transformations with congruence as they learn how to use transformations to determine congruence. If one shape can be moved in some combination of translating, rotating, or reflecting to exactly match another shape, then students can conclude that the two shapes are congruent. As students' understanding of transformations matures, they begin to realize that more than one transformation can be performed on a shape and that more than one series of transformations can be used to prove that two shapes are congruent.

Another connection that students make in grade 4 is between transformations and symmetry. For example, students can use reflections to determine whether a given shape has line symmetry. If a shape has line symmetry when it is reflected over a line, called a *line of reflection,* its image will coincide with, or appear as if it is in the same position as, the original shape. Students can use transformations to determine line symmetry by reflecting the figure and observing the resulting figure, as shown in figure 4.22.

If students trace a rectangle and the dotted line, as shown in 4.22(a), flip the paper over, and match up the dotted line, they clearly see that the "image" of the rectangle (what can be seen through the back of the paper) matches the original rectangle. Therefore, a rectangle has two lines of symmetry that are perpendicular to its sides. The reflection based on the diagonal (the dotted rectangle) shown in figure 4.22(b) illustrates that the diagonal of a rectangle is *not* a line of symmetry.

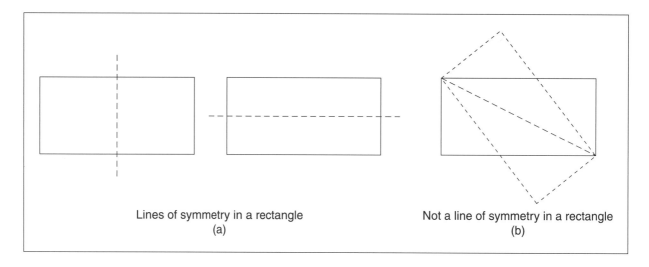

Lines of symmetry in a rectangle
(a)

Not a line of symmetry in a rectangle
(b)

Fig. 4.22. Examples illustrating how to use reflections to identify lines of symmetry

Students can use rotations to determine rotational symmetry. A shape has rotational symmetry if when rotated more than 0 degrees but fewer than 360 degrees (or one full turn), the rotated shape coincides with the original shape. The point around which the shape is rotated is called the *center of rotation,* and the angle through which it is rotated is the *angle of rotation.* Students learn that the rectangle in figure 4.23(a) has rotational symmetry because, when rotated 180 degrees (or a half-turn) about the center of the rectangle (the point at which its diagonals intersect), the rotated rectangle coincides with the original rectangle. Students can test this coincidence by tracing the rectangle, putting the point of a pencil on the point of rotation, and turning the paper around that point until the tracing matches the original rectangle. However, the trapezoid in figure 4.23(b) does not have rotational symmetry, because no rotation less than a full turn causes the rotated shape to coincide with the original shape.

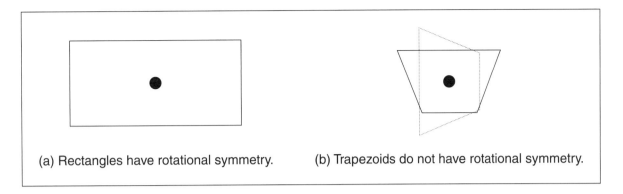

(a) Rectangles have rotational symmetry.　　(b) Trapezoids do not have rotational symmetry.

Fig. 4.23. Examples of using transformations to identify rotational symmetry

The concepts of congruence and symmetry can also be connected with area. For example, if students identify a line of symmetry in a shape, they know that the line divides the shape into two congruent parts. Students can thus infer that the area of the two parts are equal and, furthermore, that the areas of the two parts, taken together, are equal to the area of the whole shape, as shown in figure 4.24.

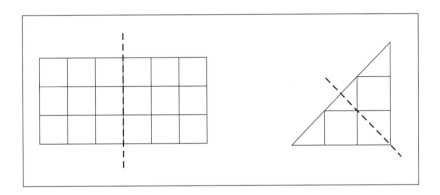

Fig. 4.24. Examples illustrating that a line of symmetry divides a figure into two congruent parts whose areas are equal.

Composing and decomposing figures to compare their areas

Students can make additional connections as they learn to compose and decompose figures to compare areas. For example, as shown in figure 4.25, as students realize that a parallelogram can be decomposed and the resulting figures recombined to form a rectangle, they begin to understand that area of the parallelogram is the same as the area of the corresponding rectangle.

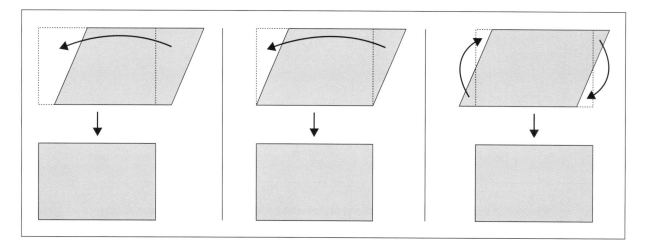

Fig. 4.25. Several ways to decompose a parallelogram and recombine the parts into a rectangle with the same area

With experiences like those illustrated in figure 4.26, students can be helped to see that two congruent triangles can be combined to create a rectangle or other type of parallelogram, and they can be asked how this idea can help them find the area of a triangle. Students will apply these informal explorations in later grades as they derive and apply area formulas.

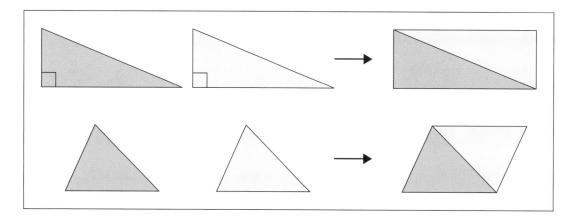

Fig. 4.26. Combining two congruent triangles to form a parallelogram that has twice as much area as the triangle

Measuring and classifying angles

In grade 4, students connect their understanding of angles and their knowledge of measurement to learn how to use a protractor to measure and draw angles of different sizes, as shown in figure 4.27. Students learn that an angle is measured in degrees and that the ° symbol is used to show degrees.

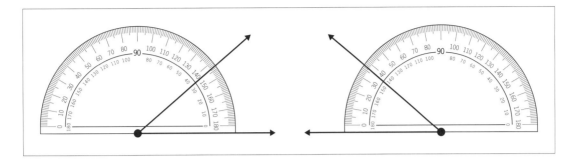

Fig. 4.27. Using a protractor to measure an angle.

Students learn that many protractors present the scale for measuring angles with two different starting points: one on the right-hand side that can be used to measure a counterclockwise opening of an angle, and one on the left-hand side that can be used to measure a clockwise opening of an angle. Activities that explore *tessellations*, or tilings of the plane, provide an interesting context in which students can deepen their understanding of angle measure and how it relates to various two-dimensional shapes. For example, as shown in figure 4.28, an arrangement of four congruent parallelograms around a common vertex can be used to completely cover the plane.

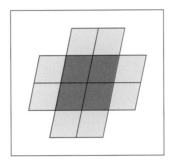

Fig. 4.28. A piece of a tessellation created with congruent parallelograms

As students investigate tessellations, they learn other combinations of congruent shapes that can be used to cover the plane, for example, six equilateral triangles around a common vertex and three hexagons around a common vertex.

Connections in Later Grades

Areas of parallelograms, triangles, and other polygons

In grade 5, students extend their exploration of area to include finding the areas of other polygons, such as triangles and parallelograms. First they learn to refer to the length and width of a rectangle as its *base* and *height*. This vocabulary facilitates students' ability to see the relationships among the formulas for the areas of rectangles and those of other polygons. Then, to understand how to find the area of other polygons, students draw on the understanding developed in grade 3 of combining and decomposing shapes. In grade 4, they learn that a parallelogram can be decomposed and its parts can be recombined to form a rectangle. In grade 5, students apply this understanding to verify that the area of a parallelogram with a base, b, and a height, h, is the same as the area of the corresponding rectangle with the same base (or length), b, and the same height (or width), h; in other words, its area can be expressed as $A = b \times h$. Students also use their informal explorations of the relationship between triangles and parallelograms, including rectangles, to verify the formula for the area of the triangle. Previously they learned that a parallelogram can be decomposed into two congruent triangles. In grade 5, students draw on this concept to discover that the area of triangle with base, b, and height, h, is equal to the half the area of the corresponding rectangle or parallelogram with the same base, b, and height, h; in other words, its area can be expressed as $A = (1/2)bh$.

Surface area and volume

As grade 4 students learn and apply their understanding of area to two-dimensional shapes, they are also laying the foundation to find surface area of three-dimensional shapes in grade 5. For example, students will learn to use their understanding of the properties of three-dimensional shapes combined with their understanding of area to realize that for the rectangular prism in figure 4.29, two of the faces are rectangles with area of 8 cm × 2 cm = 16 sq cm, two of the faces are rectangles with area of 8 cm × 3 cm = 24 sq cm, and two of the faces are rectangles with area of 3 cm × 2 cm = 6 sq cm, so the surface area of the figure can be determined as follows:

$$2(16 \text{ sq cm}) + 2(24 \text{ sq cm}) + 2(6 \text{ sq cm}) = 92 \text{ sq cm}.$$

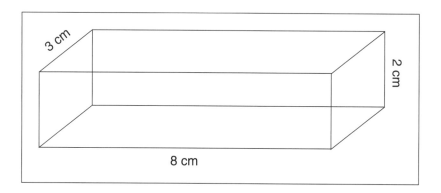

Fig. 4.29. Finding the surface area of a rectangular prism

Another connection that students make in grade 5 is the connection between area and volume. Often spatial and measurement concepts come together at different points in geometry. The exploration of volume is one of those points. Just as area was an attribute of two-dimensional space, volume is an attribute of three-dimensional space. The conceptual framework of area formed in grade 4 will give students part of the foundation they need to understand volume in grade 5. They will learn that a unit of volume is a cube that is 1 unit by 1 unit by 1 unit and that the volume of a figure is the number of those cubes that fit inside the space it surrounds, as shown in figure 4.30. Students will apply these understandings and strategies to verify the formula for the volume of a rectangular prism.

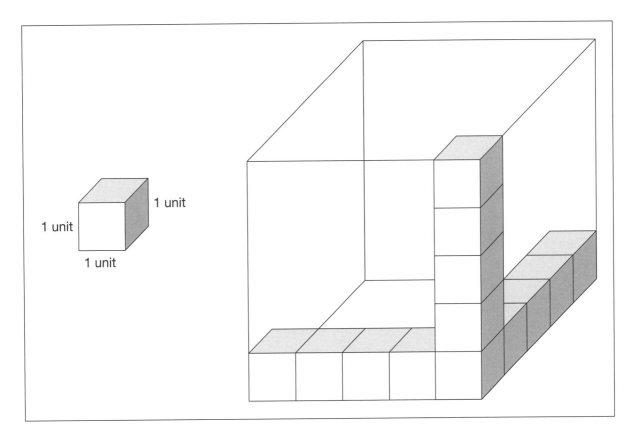

Fig. 4.30. Illustration of a unit of volume and the meaning of volume

Measuring Depth of Understanding

What are some of the essential mathematical ideas or topics that build a foundation for understanding the area of two-dimensional shapes in grade 4? How do those mathematical ideas or topics connect with learning in grade 5?

References

Donovan, M. Suzanne, and John D. Bransford, eds. *How Students Learn: Mathematics in the Classroom*. Washington, D.C.: National Research Council, 2005.

Duncan, Natalie N., Charles Geer, DeAnn Huinker, Larry Leutzinger, Ed Rathmell, and Charles Thompson. *Navigating through Number and Operations in Grades 3–5. Principles and Standards for School Mathematics* Navigations Series. Reston, Va.: National Council of Teachers of Mathematics, 2007.

Fuson, Karen C., and Aki Murata. "Integrating the NRC Principles and the NCTM Process Standards: Cognitively Guided Teaching to Individualize Instruction within Whole-Class Activities and Move All Students within Their Learning Path." *National Council of Supervisors of Mathematics Journal* 10, no. 1 (2007): 72–91.

Kilpatrick, Jeremy, Jane Swafford, and Bradford Findell. *Adding It Up: Helping Children Learn Mathematics*. Washington, D.C.: National Research Council, 2001.

Lampert, Magdalene. "Choosing and Using Mathematical Tools in Classroom Discourse." In *Advances in Research on Teaching*, vol. 1, edited by Jere Brophy, pp. 223–64. Greenwich, Conn.: JAI Press, 1989.

Mack, Nancy K. "Learning Fractions with Understanding: Building on Informal Knowledge." *Journal for Research in Mathematics Education* 21(January 1990): 16–32.

National Council of Teachers of Mathematics (NCTM). *Curriculum and Evaluation Standards for School Mathematics*. Reston, Va.: NCTM, 1989.

———. *Principles and Standards for School Mathematics*. Reston, Va.: NCTM, 2000.

———. *Curriculum Focal Points for Prekindergarten through Grade 8 Mathematics: A Quest for Coherence*. Reston, Va.: NCTM, 2006.

———. *Focus in Grade 4*. Reston, Va.: NCTM, 2009.

———. *Focus in Grade 5*. Reston, Va.: NCTM, 2009.

Additional Titles in Support of *Curriculum Focal Points for Prekindergarten through Grade 8 Mathematics*

Additional grade-level books are available from NCTM in support of *Curriculum Focal Points for Prekindergarten through Grade 8 Mathematics: A Quest for Coherence*. Readers of this book may be interested in the following titles:

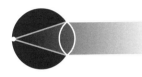

- *Focus in Grade 3: Teaching with Curriculum Focal Points;* Jane F. Schielack, Series Advisor

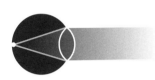

- *Focus in Grade 5: Teaching with Curriculum Focal Points;* Sybilla Beckmann, Editor

Please consult www.nctm.org/catalog for the availability of these titles, as well as for other resources for teachers of mathematics at all grade levels.

For the most up-to-date listing of NCTM resources on topics of interest to mathematics educators, as well as information on membership benefits, conferences, and workshops, visit the NCTM Web site at www.nctm.org.